MW00780148

Copy 2

AWARENESS AND PURIFICATION

AWARENESS
— AND —
PURIFICATION

Acts of the Meeting
for the Protection of
Minors in the Church

[VATICAN CITY, FEBRUARY 21-24, 2019]

TWENTY-THIRD
PUBLICATIONS
twentythirdpublications.com

TWENTY-THIRD PUBLICATIONS
One Montauk Avenue, Suite 200
New London, CT 06320
(860) 437-3012 or (800) 321-0411
www.twentythirdpublications.com

Copyright © 2019 Libreria Editrice Vaticana. All rights reserved. No part of this publication may be reproduced in any manner without prior written permission of the publisher. Write to the Permissions Editor.

Front cover photo: © iStockphoto.com / Wacharaklin
Back cover photo: © Shutterstock.com / Pajor Pawel

ISBN: 978-1-62785-476-4
Library of Congress Control Number: 2019905009
Printed in the U.S.A.

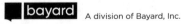 A division of Bayard, Inc.

CONTENTS

INTRODUCTION

The Courage to Give a Name to the Evil of Abuse

ANDREA TORNIELLI, *Editorial Director of*
the Dicastery for Communication of the Holy See

"Behind this is Satan." As he spoke at the end of the Mass celebrated in the Sala Regia with the 190 participants of the Meeting for the Protection of Minors in the Church, Pope Francis offered this eloquent sentence. The pope spoke boldly and realistically of a vile phenomenon. "In these painful cases," he said, "I see the hand of evil that does not spare even the innocence of the little ones. And this leads me to think of the example of Herod who, driven by fear of losing his power, ordered the slaughter of all the children of Bethlehem." Previously, during an interview with journalists on an airplane, Francis had compared the abuse to "a black mass." So "behind this is Satan," the hand of evil.

Recognizing this does not mean forgetting all explanations or diminishing the personal responsibilities of institutions, individuals, or groups. It does not mean closing one's eyes to the need for increasingly safe and transparent protocols and laws, for acting against abusers, or for secure environments. It means situating all this in a deeper context, understanding its true origin.

For four days, February 21-24, 2019, bishops from all over the world representing the entire world episcopate, together with representatives of the superiors of male and female religious orders and some lay people, met with Peter to become more aware of the tragedy of victims of abuse and to work together on responsibility, accountability, and transparency.

In his concluding address, the pope spoke of abuses not only in the Church, but also in the world. He did this to manifest the concern of a father and pastor, not to minimize the seriousness of the abuses perpetrated in the ecclesial context, because, he said, "the brutality of this worldwide phenomenon becomes all the more grave and scandalous in the Church." Parents who had entrusted their children to priests, to introduce them to the life of faith, saw them return irreparably and permanently wounded in body and soul. In the justified anger of these people, the pope said, "the Church sees the reflection of the wrath of God, betrayed and insulted by these deceitful consecrated persons."

The silent cry of the abused, the incurable tragedy of their lives destroyed by the consecrated men turned into corrupt and insensitive orcs, resounded loudly in the synod hall in those days of late February. It pierced the hearts of bishops and religious superiors. It swept away justifications and helped to put legal and technical aspects in the proper perspective. The universal Church became aware of the absolute gravity of the phenomenon as never before, because the representatives of the entire world episcopate had never met to discuss this topic. Nor has the voice of survivors ever sounded so dramatically and repeatedly, as happened in the synod hall in those days, with their testimonies included in the context of evening prayer at the end of each day.

Pope Francis, concluding the meeting, thanked the many priests and religious who spend themselves to proclaim the Gospel and to educate and protect the little ones and the helpless by giving their lives in the following of Jesus. Looking into the abyss of evil can never make us forget the good, not out of useless pride but because one needs to know where to look and who to follow as an example.

But the meeting in the Vatican, which one can follow day by day through these pages, was not just a punch to the gut that made the participants more conscious of the devastating action of evil and sin and therefore of the need to ask forgiveness by invoking the help of divine grace. The summit also attested to the firm intention to give substance to what emerged with effective operational action, because the awareness of the gravity of sin and the constant appeal to heaven for help, which characterized the meeting at the Vatican, go hand in hand with a renewed operational commitment to ensure that ecclesial environments will become always safer for minors and vulnerable adults, in the hope that this commitment can also spread to all other sectors of our societies.

FEBRUARY 21, 2019

Responsibility

OPENING REMARKS OF
HIS HOLINESS POPE FRANCIS

Dear Brothers, good morning!

In light of the scourge of sexual abuse perpetrated by ecclesiastics to the great harm of minors, I wanted to consult you, Patriarchs, Cardinals, Archbishops, Bishops, and Religious Superiors and Leaders, so that together we might listen to the Holy Spirit and, in docility to his guidance, hear the cry of the little ones who plead for justice. In this meeting, we sense the weight of the pastoral and ecclesial responsibility that obliges us to discuss together, in a synodal, frank, and in-depth manner, how to confront this evil afflicting the Church and humanity. The holy People of God looks to us, and expects from us not simple and predictable condemnations, but concrete and effective measures to be undertaken. We need to be concrete.

So we begin this process armed with faith and a spirit of great *parrhesia*, courage, and concreteness.

As a help, I would share with you some important criteria formulated by the various Episcopal Commissions and Conferences—they came from you and I have organized them somewhat. They are guidelines to assist in our reflection, and they will now be distributed to you. They are a simple point of departure that came from you and now return to you. They are not meant to detract from the creativity needed in this meeting.

In your name, I would also like to thank the Pontifical Commission for the Protection of Minors, the Congregation for the Doctrine of the Faith, and the members of the Organizing Committee for their outstanding and dedicated work in preparing for this meeting. Many thanks!

Finally, I ask the Holy Spirit to sustain us throughout these days, and to help us to turn this evil into an opportunity for awareness and purification. May the Virgin Mary enlighten us as we seek to heal the grave wounds that the scandal of pedophilia has caused, both in the little ones and in believers.

Thank you.

POINTS FOR REFLECTION[1]

1. Prepare a practical handbook indicating the steps to be taken by authorities at key moments when a case emerges.

2. Establish listening structures that include trained and expert people who can initially discern the cases of the alleged victims.

3. Establish the criteria for the direct involvement of the bishop or of the religious superior.

4. Implement shared procedures for the examination of the charges, the protection of the victims, and the right of defense of the accused.

5. Inform the civil authorities and the higher ecclesiastical authorities in compliance with civil and canonical norms.

6. Make a periodic review of protocols and norms to safeguard a protected environment for minors in all pastoral structures: protocols and norms based on the integrated principles of justice and charity so that the action of the Church in this matter is in conformity with her mission.

7. Establish specific protocols for handling accusations against bishops.

8. Accompany, protect, and treat victims, offering them all the necessary support for a complete recovery.

9. Increase awareness of the causes and consequences of sexual abuse through ongoing formation initiatives of bishops, religious superiors, clerics, and pastoral workers.

10. Prepare pathways of pastoral care for communities injured by abuses and paths of penance and recovery for the perpetrators.

---

1   These points were formulated by the various Commissions and Episcopal Conferences as a guide for reflection during the course of the Meeting for the Protection of Minors in the Church.

11. Consolidate the collaboration with all people of good will and with the operators of mass media in order to recognize and discern real cases from false ones and accusations of slander, avoiding rancor and insinuations, rumors and defamation (cf. Pope Francis' Address to the Roman Curia, 21 December 2018).

12. Raise the minimum age for marriage to sixteen years.

13. Establish policies that regulate and facilitate the participation of lay experts in investigations and in the different degrees of judgment of canonical processes concerning sexual and / or abuse of power.

14. The right to defense: the principle of presumption of innocence, supported by both natural law and canon law, must also be safeguarded until the guilt of the accused is proven. Therefore, it is necessary to prevent the lists of the accused being published, even by the dioceses, before preliminary investigation and definitive condemnation.

15. Observe the traditional principle of proportionality of punishment with respect to the crime committed. To decide that priests and bishops guilty of sexual abuse of minors leave the public ministry.

16. Introduce rules concerning seminarians and candidates for the priesthood or religious life. Be sure that there are programs of initial and ongoing formation to help them develop their human, spiritual, and psychosexual maturity, as well as their interpersonal relationships and their behavior.

17. Be sure to have psychological evaluations by qualified and accredited experts for candidates for the priesthood and consecrated life.

18. Establish norms governing the transfer of a seminarian or religious aspirant from one seminary to another; as well as a priest or religious from one diocese or congregation to another.

19. Formulate mandatory codes of conduct for all clerics, religious, service personnel, and volunteers to outline appropriate boundaries in personal relationships. Be specific about the necessary requirements for staff and volunteers and check their criminal record.

20. Explain all information and data on the dangers of abuse and its effects, on how to recognize signs of abuse, and on how to report suspected sexual abuse. All this must take place in collaboration with parents, teachers, professionals, and civil authorities.

21. Where it is not yet in place, establish an easily accessible organization for victims who want to report any crimes. Such an organization should have a certain autonomy with respect to the local ecclesiastical authority and include expert persons (clerics and laity) who know how to express the Church's attention to those who have been offended by improper attitudes on the part of clerics.

TESTIMONIALS

OF VICTIMS OF

SEXUAL ABUSE

FIRST TESTIMONY

First of all, I want to thank the Commission for allowing me to address you today and the Holy Father for all the support and help he has given us in recent times. They asked me to talk about the pain that comes from sexual abuse. Everyone knows that sexual abuse leaves tremendous consequences for everyone. I therefore believe that it is not worthwhile to continue to talk about this because the consequences are evident in all aspects, and they persist for the rest of one's life.

Instead I would like to speak about myself as a Catholic, about what happened to me, and about what I would like to say to the bishops. For a Catholic, the most difficult thing is to be able to speak about sexual abuse; but once you have taken courage and begun telling—in our case, I speak of myself—the first thing I thought was: I'm going to tell everything to Holy Mother Church, where they will listen to me and respect me. The first thing they did was to treat me as a liar, turn their backs and tell me that I, and others, were enemies of the Church. This pattern exists not only in Chile: it exists all over the world, and this must end.

I know that there has been talk about how to end this phenomenon, how to prevent it from happening again, and how to eliminate this evil. First of all: false forgiveness, forced forgiveness does not work. Victims need to be believed, respected, cared for, and healed. You need to repair what has been done to the victims, be close to them, believe them, and accompany them. You are the physicians of the soul and yet, with rare exceptions, you have been transformed—in some cases—into murderers of the soul, into murderers of the faith. What a terrible contradiction. I wonder: What does Jesus think? What does Mary think, when she sees that it is her own shepherds who betray their own little sheep? I ask you, please collaborate with justice, because you have a special care for the victims, so that what is happening in Chile, that is, what the pope is doing in Chile, may be repeated as a model in other countries of the world.

We see the tip of the iceberg every day: although the Church says it's all over, cases continue to emerge. Why? Because it proceeds like when you are diagnosed with a tumor: you must treat the whole cancer, not just remove the tumor, so you need chemotherapy, radiotherapy, you need to have some treatment. It is not enough to remove the tumor and that's it. I ask you to listen to what the Holy Father wants to do, not limiting yourself to nodding your head and then doing something else. The only thing I ask of you—and I ask the Holy Spirit—is to help restore that trust in the Church, that those who do not want to listen to the Holy Spirit and who want to continue to cover-up leave the Church in order to make way for those who want to create a new Church, a renewed Church, and a Church absolutely free from sexual abuse. I entrust all this to the Virgin, to the Lord, that all this may become a reality. We cannot continue with this crime of covering the scourge of sexual abuse in the Church. I hope that the Lord and Mary will enlighten you and that, once and for all, we work with justice to remove this cancer from the Church, because it is destroying it. And this is what the devil wants. Thank you.

SECOND TESTIMONY

Q. What hurt you most in life?

R. From the age of fifteen I had sexual relations with a priest. This lasted for thirteen years. I got pregnant three times and he made me have an abortion three times, quite simply because he did not want to use condoms or contraceptives. At first I trusted him so much that I did not know he could abuse me. I was afraid of him, and every time I refused to have sex with him, he would beat me. And since I was completely dependent on him economically, I suffered all the humiliations he inflicted on me. We had these relations both in his home in the village and in the diocesan reception center. In this relationship I did not have the right to have "boyfriends"; whenever I had one and he came to know about it, he would beat me up. That was the condition for helping me economically. He gave me everything I wanted, when I accepted to have sex; otherwise he would beat me.

Q. How did you deal with these wounds and how do you feel now?

R. I feel I have a life destroyed. I have suffered so many humiliations in this relationship that I do not know what the future holds for me…. This made me very cautious in my relationships, now.

Q. What message do you want to pass to the bishops?

R. It must be said that to love, essentially is to love freely: when a person loves someone you think of their future, of their good. You cannot abuse a person this way. It must be said that priests and religious are able to help and at the same time to destroy: they have to behave like leaders, like wise people.

Q. Thank you very much. Your contribution will be very significant for the bishops' Meeting. Once again, thank you.

THIRD TESTIMONY

I am fifty-three years old. I am a religious priest. This year is the twenty-fifth since my ordination. I am grateful to God. What hurt me? An encounter with a priest hurt me. As a teenager, after my conversion, I went to the priest so he could teach me how to read Scriptures during Mass; and he touched my private parts. I spent a night in his bed. This hurt me deeply. The other thing that hurt me was the bishop to whom, after many years, as an adult, I talked about the incident. I went to him together with my provincial. First, I wrote a letter to the bishop, and six months later, I had a meeting with the priest. The bishop did not answer me, and after six months, I wrote to the nuncio. The nuncio reacted showing understanding. Then I met the bishop and he attacked me without trying to understand me, and this hurt me. On the one hand the priest, and on the other, this bishop who… *What do I feel?* I feel bad, because neither that priest nor the bishop answered my letter, and it's been eight years and he has not even answered. What would I like to say to the bishops? That they listen to these people; that they learn to listen to the people who speak. I wanted someone to listen to me, to know who that man, that priest, is and what he does. I forgive that priest and the bishop from the heart. I thank God for the Church, I am grateful to be in the Church. I have many priest friends who have helped me.

FOURTH TESTIMONY

Hello. I appreciate this outreach to survivors of clergy sexual abuse, and I am happy to participate in this project.

What has wounded me the most? As I reflect on that question, I think back to the total… to the full realization of the total loss of the innocence of my youth and how that has affected me today.

There's still pain in my family relationships. There's still pain with my siblings. I still carry pain. My parents still carry pain at the dysfunction, the betrayal, the manipulation that this evil man, who was our Catholic priest at the time, wrought upon my family and myself.

So that's what has wounded me the most and what I carry with me today.

I am doing well now because I have found hope and healing by telling my story, by sharing my story with my family, my wife and my children, my extended family, my friends, and because I can do that, I feel more comfortable with myself and how I can be myself.

And finally, what I want to tell the bishops—I think that's an excellent question: I would ask the bishops for leadership. Leadership and vision and courage.

That's what I respond to, that's what I hope to see. I have a personal experience of leadership and how it has affected me personally. One of my finest memories of Francis Cardinal George is when he spoke about the difficulties of fellow priests who have abused, and I considered those words, coming from a man in his position, even though they must be really hard for him to say, they were the right and proper thing to say. I thought that was leadership at the time, and I think it's leadership now. And I thought if he could put himself out there, and lead by example, then I could put myself out there and I think other survivors and other Catholics and faithful people can put themselves out there, to work for resolution, and work for healing, and work for a better Church.

So we respond to leadership, we look to our bishops for leadership. I would ask the bishops to show leadership.

FIFTH TESTIMONY

I was sexually molested for a long time, over a hundred times, and this sexual molestation has created traumas and flashbacks all across my life. It's difficult to live life; it's difficult to be with people, to get connected with people. I carried an attitude for my family, for my friends, and even for God.

Every time I have spoken to the provincials and to the major superiors, they have all practically covered every issue, covered the perpetrators and that kills me sometimes. It's been a long time that I have been fighting this battle… and most of the superiors are not able to stop the abusers because of the friendships among them.

I'll request the provincials as well as the major superiors and the bishops sitting in this audience to make strong acts which really put the perpetrator into place. If we want to save the Church, I think the perpetrators need to be punished.

I'll request the bishops to get their act clear because this is one of the time bombs happening in the Church of Asia. If we want to save the Church, we need to put our act together and make public the names of the perpetrators. We must not allow friendships to prevail, because this will destroy an entire generation of children. As Jesus said, we need to be child-like, not to be child sexual molesters.

PRESENTATIONS

THE SMELL OF THE SHEEP

*Knowing Their Pain and Healing Their Wounds
Is at the Core of the Shepherd's Task*

CARDINAL LUIS ANTONIO G. TAGLE, *Archbishop of Manila,
President of Caritas International*

The abuse of minors by ordained ministers has inflicted wounds not only on the victims, but also on their families, the clergy, the Church, the wider society, the perpetrators themselves, and the bishops. But it is also true, we humbly and sorrowfully admit, that wounds have been inflicted by us bishops on the victims and in fact the entire body of Christ. Our lack of response to the suffering of victims, even to the point of rejecting them and covering up the scandal to protect perpetrators and the institution has injured our people, leaving a deep wound in our relationship with those we are sent to serve. People are rightly asking, "Have you, who are called to have the smell of the sheep upon you, not instead run away when you found the stench of the filth inflicted on children and vulnerable people you were supposed to protect, too strong to endure?" Wounds call for healing. But what does healing consist in? How do we as bishops, who have been part of the wounding, now promote healing in this specific context? The theme of healing of wounds has been the subject of many inter-disciplinary studies. And I cannot pretend to know all the findings of the human and social sciences on the subject, but I believe we need to recover and maintain a faith and ecclesial perspective to guide us. I repeat: a faith and ecclesial perspective to guide us, as stressed many times by Pope Francis. For my presentation, especially the first part, I invite everyone to look to the Risen Lord and learn from him, his disciples, and their encounter.[1]

---

1   I want to acknowledge at this point the studies published by Roberto Goizueta, Richard Horsley, Barbara Reid, Tomas Halik, Robert Enright, and Cardinal Albert Vanhoye, to name a few authors, who have helped me in my reflection.

The apparition of the Risen Lord to the disciples and to Thomas (John 20:19–28)

St. John's Gospel narrates an apparition of the Risen Lord to the disciples on the evening of the first day of the week. The doors were locked as the disciples cowered in fear, wondering if they would be the next to be arrested and crucified. It is in this moment of utter helplessness that the risen and yet still wounded Jesus stands in their midst. After greeting them with the message of the resurrection, "Peace be with you," he showed them his hands and his side, marked by gaping wounds. Only by drawing close to his wounds could they be sent on a mission of reconciliation and forgiveness by the power of the Holy Spirit. Thomas was not with them at that time. Let us now hear the account of the encounter between the Risen Lord and Thomas.

> Thomas, called Didymus, one of the Twelve, was not with them when Jesus came. So, the other disciples said to him, "We have seen the Lord." But he said to them, "Unless I see the mark of the nails in his hands and put my finger into the nail marks and put my hand into his side, I will not believe." Now a week later his disciples were again inside the room and Thomas was with them. Jesus came, although the doors were locked, and stood in their midst and said, "Peace be with you." Then he said to Thomas, "Put your finger here and see my hands, and bring your hand and put it into my side, and do not be unbelieving, but believe." Thomas answered and said to him, "My Lord and my God!"

Those sent must be in touch with wounded humanity

Notice how Jesus invites them again to look at his wounds. He even insists that Thomas put his finger into the wounds of his hands and to bring his hand into the wound of his side. Try to imagine how Thomas must have felt. But from seeing the wounds of the Risen Lord, he makes the supreme profession of faith in Jesus as Lord and God. Seeing and touching the wounds of Jesus are fundamental to the act and confession of faith. What can we learn from this intimate encounter? By repeating this action twice, the evangelist makes clear that those who are sent to proclaim the core of our Christian faith, the dying and rising of Christ, can only do so with authenticity if they are constantly in touch with the wounds of humanity. That is one of the marks of our ministry. This is true of Thomas, and it is true of the Church of all time, especially in our time. Msgr. Tomas Halik writes, "Christ comes to him, to Thomas, and shows him His wounds. This means that the resurrection is not the 'effacement' or devaluation of the cross. Wounds remain wounds." The wounds of Christ remain in the wounds of our world. And Msgr. Halik adds, "Our world is full of wounds. It is my conviction that those who close their eyes to the wounds in our world have no right to say, 'My Lord and my God.'" For him, seeing and touching the wounds of Christ in the wounds of humanity is a condition for authentic faith. He further says, "I cannot believe until I touch the wounds, the suffering of the world—for all the painful wounds, all the misery of the world and of humankind are Christ's wounds! I do not have the right to confess God unless I take seriously my neighbor's pain. Faith that would like to close its eyes to people's suffering is just an illusion." Faith is born and reborn only from the wounds of the Crucified and Risen Christ seen and touched in the wounds of humankind. Only a wounded faith is credible (Halik). How can we profess faith in Christ when we close our eyes to all the wounds inflicted by abuse?

What is at stake

Brothers and sisters, this is what is at stake at this moment of crisis brought about by the abuse of children and our poor handling of these crimes. Our people need us to draw close to their wounds and acknowledge our faults if we are to give authentic and credible witness to our faith in the Resurrection. This means that each of us and our brothers and sisters at home must take personal responsibility for bringing healing to this wound in the body of Christ and make the commitment to do everything in our power and capacity to see that children are safe, are cared for in our communities.

The presence of the wounds of the crucifixion on the Risen Lord, for me, defies human logic. If the world were in charge of choreographing the resurrection, Jesus would have showed up at Herod's house or Pilate's porch and made it the biggest "I told you so" in history. Jesus would have manifested his final triumph by eliminating all signs of pain, injustice, and defeat. Let all of them be buried in the dark past and never be resurrected. But that is not the way of Jesus Christ. The resurrection is not an illusionary victory. By showing his wounds to the disciples, Jesus restores their memory. Roberto Goizueta justly comments that "the wounds on Christ's glorified body are the incarnated memory of the relationships that defined his life and death." The wounds of Jesus are the consequence of his loving and compassionate relationship with the poor, the sick, tax collectors, women of ill repute, persons afflicted with leprosy, noisy children, outsiders, and foreigners. The wounds of Jesus are the consequence of his allowing himself to be wounded as he touched the wounds of others. He was crucified because he loved these concrete persons who were themselves wounded by society and religion. By sharing in their weakness and wounds, he became a compassionate brother rather than a harsh judge. So the letter to the Hebrews 5:8–9 affirms, "Son though he was, he learned obedience from what he suffered, and when he was made perfect, he became the source of eternal salvation for all who obey him." So the wounds of the Risen Lord remind the disciples of the love that is ready to be wounded out of compassion for humankind. His wounds are the wounds of others that he freely bore. He did not inflict wounds on others, but he was ready to be wounded by his love for and communion with them. As Frederick Gaiser said, "The healing shepherd is never far from dangers, never impervious to the evils and infirmities from which he seeks to protect the flock." Only the wounds of love and compassion can heal.

Do not be afraid

My dear brothers and sisters, we need to put aside any hesitation to draw close to the wounds of our people out of fear of being wounded ourselves. Yes, much of the wounds we will suffer are part of the restoration of memory we must undergo, as did those disciples of Jesus. The wounds of the Risen Lord reminded the disciples of betrayal, their own betrayal and abandonment of Jesus when they saved their own lives out of fear. They fled at the first moment of danger, afraid of the cost of discipleship, and in Peter's case, even denying that he even knew the Lord. Jesus' wounds also remind them and us that wounds are often inflicted by blindness of ambition and legalism and misuse of power that condemned an innocent person to die as a criminal. The wounds of the Risen Christ carry the memory of innocent suffering, but they also carry the memory of our weakness and sinfulness.

If we want to be agents of healing, let us reject any tendency that is part of worldly thinking that refuses to see and touch the wounds of others, which are Christ's wounds in the wounded people. Those wounded by abuse and the scandal need us to be strong in faith in this moment. The world needs authentic witnesses to the resurrection of Jesus who draw close to his wounds as the first act of faith. I will be stressing: this is an act of faith.

Roberto Goizueta claims that the denial of wounds and death leads to the death of others and to our own death. There is great fear today in the hearts of people, and indeed in our own hearts, that cause humanity in our time to shun touching the wounds in our world simply because we are afraid of facing our own wounds, our own mortality, weakness, sinfulness, and vulnerability. Ernest Becker observes that we avoid pain and suffering as unwanted reminders that we are vulnerable. We are fooled into believing that having much money, the right insurance policy, the strictest security, closed circuit television cameras, the latest models of cars and gadgets, and membership in rejuvenating health clubs could make us immortal. Sadly, we do also eliminate the wounded in our midst by getting them out of the streets when dignitaries visit or by covering their shanties with painted walls. Goizueta poignantly says, "If we deny death, we inflict it. If we deny death, we will inflict death. But we also inflict it on ourselves. The fear of pain and vulnerability that causes us to shun real human relationships, to shun that true love that always involves surrender and vulnerability in the face of another, ultimately kills our—our!—interior life, our ability to feel anything—neither pain nor joy, nor love." Our capacity to love might die. The fear of wounds isolates us and makes us indifferent to the needs of others. Fear drives people to violent and irrational behavior. Fear motivates people to defend themselves even when no threats exist. Those who sow fear in others and society are actually afraid of themselves. In the Risen Jesus we know that by seeing and touching the wounds of those who suffer, we touch our own wounds and we touch Jesus. We become brothers and sisters to one another. We acknowledge our common guilt in inflicting wounds on humankind and creation. We hear the call to reconciliation. We see the patient presence of the Risen Lord in our broken world.

Continual accompaniment in solidarity

The second and last part of my sharing consists in a psychologist's proposal on how to address the crisis in the light of faith. For this portion I will rely heavily on Dr. Robert Enright, professor at the University of Wisconsin-Madison in the United States and the pioneer in the social scientific study of forgiveness. We are collaborating with him on the program of forgiveness in the Philippines. In fact, in this very moment there is a session among Catholic school educators in Manila on "Pain, Wound and Forgiveness." According to Dr. Enright, one concern that we must address is: Once justice is served, how do we help the victims to heal from the effects of the abuse? Justice is necessary, but by itself does not heal the broken human heart. If we are to serve the victims and all those wounded by the crisis, we need to take seriously their wound of resentment and pain and the need for healing. Resentment can be like a disease that slowly and steadily infects people, until their enthusiasm and energy are gone. With increasing stress, they are prone to heightened anxiety and depression, lowered self-images, and interpersonal conflicts that arise from the inner brokenness. Yet before we even raise the issue of asking the victims to forgive as part of their healing, we must clarify that we are not suggesting that they should just let it all go, excuse the abuse, just move on. No. Far from it. Without question, we know that when victims come to a moment of forgiving others who have harmed them, a deeper healing takes place and the understandable resentments that build up in their hearts are reconciled. We know that forgiveness is one powerful and even scientifically supported pathway for eliminating pain and resentment in the human heart. We as the Church should continue to walk with those profoundly wounded by abuse, building trust, providing unconditional love, and repeatedly asking for forgiveness in the full recognition that we do not deserve that forgiveness in the order of justice but can only receive it when it is bestowed as gift and grace in the process of healing.

Finally, we are concerned that in some cases bishops and religious superiors are tempted—perhaps even at times pressured—to choose between victim and perpetrator. Who should we be helping? Who should be helped? Now, a focus on justice and forgiveness shows us the answer: We focus on both. Regarding victims, we need to help them to express their deep hurts and to heal from them. Regarding the perpetrators, we need to serve justice, help them to face the truth without rationalization, and at the same time not neglect their inner world, their own wounds.

At times, we are tempted to think in "either/or" terms: We strive either for justice or we try to offer forgiveness. We need a shift to a "both/and" stance as we deliberately ask these questions: How can we serve justice and foster forgiveness in the face of this wound of sexual abuse? How can we prevent distorting forgiveness so that we do not equate it with just letting the injustice slide away or move on and dismiss the wrong? How can we keep an accurate view of forgiveness as offering a startling mercy of unconditional love to those who have done wrong, while at the same time, we strive for justice? How can we renew the Church by a firm correction of a definite wrong and walk with the abused, patiently and repeatedly begging forgiveness, knowing that giving such a gift can heal them even more?

Conclusion

By way of conclusion, I would like to read a portion from Pope Francis's "Letter to the Pilgrim People of God in Chile" (May 31, 2018): "Without this vision of faith, anything we could say or do would fail. This certainty is essential to look at the present without evasiveness but with audacity, with courage but wisely, with tenacity but without violence, with passion but without fanaticism, with constancy but without anxiety, and so to change everything that today can put at risk the integrity and dignity of each person. Indeed, the solutions we need require that problems be tackled without getting caught up in it or, worse still, repeating the same mechanisms they want to eliminate" (n. 2).

Learning from the Risen Lord and his disciples, we look at and touch the wounds of victims, families, guilty and innocent clergy, the Church, and society. Beholding Jesus wounded by betrayal and abuse of power, we see the wounds of those hurt by those who should have protected them. In Jesus we experience the mercy that preserves justice and celebrates the gift of forgiveness. The Church hopefully would be a community of justice coming from communion and compassion, a Church eager to go forth on a mission of reconciliation to the wounded world in the Holy Spirit. Once again, the Crucified and Risen Lord stands in our midst at this moment, shows us his wounds and proclaims, "Peace be with you!" May we ever grow in our faith in this great mystery. Thank you.

TAKING RESPONSIBILITY

For Processing Cases of Sexual Abuse Crisis
and for Prevention of Abuse

ARCHBISHOP CHARLES J. SCICLUNA, *Archbishop of Malta,*
Adjunct Secretary of the Congregation for the Doctrine of the Faith

Introduction

The way we bishops exercise our ministry at the service of justice in our communities is one of the fundamental tests of our stewardship and, indeed, of our fidelity. To quote the Lord in Luke 12:48: "Everyone to whom much is given, of him will much be required; and of him to whom men commit much, they will demand more." We have been entrusted with the care of our people. It is our sacred duty to protect our people and to ensure justice when they have been abused.

In his letter to the People of God in Ireland, issued on March 19, 2010, Pope Benedict XVI had this to say:

> Only by examining carefully the many elements that gave rise to the present crisis can a clear-sighted diagnosis of its causes be undertaken and effective remedies be found. Certainly, among the contributing factors we can include: inadequate procedures for determining the suitability of candidates for the priesthood and the religious life; insufficient human, moral, intellectual and spiritual formation in seminaries and novitiates; a tendency in society to favor the clergy and other authority figures; and a misplaced concern for the reputation of the Church and the avoidance of scandal, resulting in failure to apply existing canonical penalties and to safeguard the dignity of every person. Urgent action is needed to address these factors, which have had such tragic consequences in the lives of victims and

their families, and have obscured the light of the Gospel to a degree that not even centuries of persecution succeeded in doing. (n. 4b)

My address this morning intends to go through the main phases of processes of individual cases of sexual abuse of minors by members of the clergy with some practical suggestions dictated by prudence, best practice, and the paramount concern for the safeguarding of the innocence of our children and young people.

Reporting sexual misconduct

The first phase is the *reporting of sexual misconduct.*

It is essential that the community be advised that they have the duty and the right to report sexual misconduct to a contact person in the diocese or religious order. These contact details should be in the public domain. It is advisable that if and when a case of misconduct is referred directly to the bishop or religious superior, they refer the information to the designated contact person.

In every case and for all the phases of dealing with cases, these two points should be followed at all times: i) protocols established should be respected; ii) civil or domestic laws should be obeyed. It is important that every allegation is investigated with the help of experts and that the investigation is concluded without unnecessary delay. The discernment of the ecclesiastical authority should be collegial. In a number of local churches, review boards or safeguarding commissions have been established, and this experience has proved to be beneficial.

It is such a relief for us bishops when we are able to share our sorrow, our pain and frustration as we face the terrible effects of the misconduct of some of our priests. Expert advice brings light and comfort and helps us arrive at decisions that are based on scientific and professional competence. Tackling cases as they arise in a synodal or collegial setting will give the necessary energy to bishops to reach out in a pastoral way to the victims, the accused priests, the community of the faithful, and indeed to society at large. All these persons require special attention, and the bishop and religious superior needs to extend his pastoral solicitude to them either in person or through his delegates. As shepherds of the Lord's flock, we should not underestimate the need to confront ourselves with the deep wounds inflicted on victims of sex abuse by members of the clergy. They are wounds of a psychological and spiritual nature that need tending with care. In my many meetings with victims around the world, I have come to realize that this is sacred ground where we meet Jesus on the Cross. This is a Via Crucis we bishops and other Church leaders cannot miss. We need to be Simon of Cyrene helping victims, with whom Jesus identifies himself (Matthew 25), carry their heavy cross.

Investigating cases of sexual misconduct

According to the motu propio *Sacramentorum Sanctitatis Tutela*, the result of the investigation of sexual misconduct of clergy with minors under the age of eighteen years should be referred to the Congregation for the Doctrine of Faith. In these cases, the Ordinary is authorized by canon law to apply precautionary measures (CIC, c. 1722) limiting or prohibiting the exercise of ministry. The Ordinary should consult his canonical experts in all cases of sexual misconduct so that referral is done when it needs to be done and proper procedures are adopted on the local level when the case is not reserved to the Holy See (for example, when misconduct occurs between consenting adults). Experts will furthermore help the bishop or religious superior share all the necessary information with the CDF and will help him express his advice on the merits of the allegations and the procedures to be adopted. It is advisable that the Ordinary follow up the case with the CDF. The bishop or religious superior is best placed to discern the potential impact of the outcome of the case on his community. The CDF takes the advice of the bishop seriously and is always available to discuss individual cases with the competent ecclesiastical authorities.

Canonical penal processes

In most cases referred to the CDF, a canonical penal process is authorized by the Holy See. The majority of canonical penal processes are of the extra-judicial or administrative type (CIC, c. 1720). Judicial penal processes are authorized in a lesser number of cases. In both types of process, the Ordinary has the duty to nominate Delegates and Assessors or Judges and Promoters of Justice that are prudent, academically qualified, and renowned for their sense of fairness. In our system, as it obtains at the present, the role of the victim of sexual abuse in canonical proceedings is limited. The pastoral solicitude of the Ordinary will help make up for this lacuna.

The person responsible for safeguarding in the diocese or the religious order should be able to share information on the progress of the proceedings with the victim or the victims in the case. In the judicial penal process, the victim has the right to institute a case for damages before the ecclesiastical judge of First Instance. In the case of an administrative penal process this initiative should be taken by the Ordinary on behalf of the victim, requesting the Delegate to award damages in favor of the victim as a subordinate consequence of an eventual decision of guilt. The essence of a just process requires that the accused is presented with all arguments and evidence against him; that the accused is given the full benefit of the right of presenting his defense; that judgment is given based on the facts of the case and the law applicable to the case; that a reasoned judgment or decision is communicated in writing to the accused and that the accused enjoy a remedy against a judgment or decision that aggrieves him.

Once the Ordinary, following the instructions of the CDF, nominates a Delegate and his Assessors in an administrative process, or nominates the members of the tribunal in a judicial penal process, he should let the persons nominated do their work and should refrain from interfering in the process. It remains his duty, however, to ensure that the process is done in a timely manner and according to canon law. A canonical penal process, whether judicial or administrative, ends with one of three possible outcomes: a *decisio condemnatoria* (where the reus is found guilty of a canonical delict); a *decisio dimissoria* (where the accusations have not been proven); or a *decisio absolutoria* (where the accused is declared innocent). A *decisio dimissoria* may create a dilemma.

The bishop or religious superior may still be uncomfortable with reassigning the accused to ministry in a case where the allegations are credible but the case has not been proven. Expert advice is essential in these cases, and the Ordinary should use his authority to guarantee the common good and ensure the effective safeguarding of children and young people.

The interface with civil jurisdiction

An essential aspect of the exercise of stewardship in these cases is the proper interface with civil jurisdiction. We are talking about misconduct that is also a crime in all civil jurisdictions. The competence of the state authorities should be respected. Reporting laws should be followed carefully, and a spirit of collaboration will benefit both the Church and society in general.

The civil courts have jurisdiction to punish crime and another jurisdiction to award damages under laws concerning civil matters. Civil thresholds or criteria of proof may be different from those exercised in canonical proceedings. The difference of outcomes for the same case is not a rare occurrence. In a number of canonical proceedings, the acts presented or produced during civil proceedings are presented as an element of proof. This happens quite frequently in cases of the acquisition, possession, or divulging of pornography featuring minors where the State authorities possess better means of detection, surveillance, and access to evidence. The difference in laws concerning the statute of limitations or prescription is another motive for a diversity of outcomes in the same case decided under different jurisdictions. The power of the CDF to derogate from the twenty-year prescription is still invoked in a number of historical cases, but admittedly this should not be the norm but rather the exception. The *ratio legis* here is that the establishment of the truth and the guarantee of justice require the possibility of the exercise of judicial jurisdiction in favor of the common good even in cases where the crime was committed a long time ago.

Implementing canonical decisions

The bishop and the religious superior have the duty to supervise the implementation and execution of the legitimate outcomes of penal proceedings. Allowance has to be made for the right of the accused to resort to the remedies allowed by law against a decision that aggrieves him. Once the appeal stage is exhausted, it is the duty of the Ordinary to inform the Community of the definitive outcome of the process. Decisions that declare the guilt of the accused and the punishment imposed should be implemented without delay. Decisions that declare the innocence of the accused should also be given due publicity. We all know that it is very difficult to restore the good name of a priest who may have been unjustly accused. The question of aftercare in these cases also involves the care of victims who have been betrayed in the most fundamental and spiritual aspects of their personality and their being. Their families are also deeply affected, and the whole community should share the burden of their grief and move together with them toward healing.

The words of Benedict XVI to the bishops of Ireland on October 28, 2006 sound the more prophetic today:

> In the exercise of your pastoral ministry, you have had to respond in recent years to many heart-rending cases of sexual abuse of minors. These are all the more tragic when the abuser is a cleric. The wounds caused by such acts run deep, and it is an urgent task to rebuild confidence and trust where these have been damaged. In your continuing efforts to deal effectively with this problem, it is important to establish the truth of what happened in the past, to take whatever steps are necessary to prevent it from occurring again, to ensure that the principles of justice are fully respected and, above all, to bring healing to the victims and to all those affected by these egregious crimes. In this way, the Church in Ireland will grow stronger and be ever more capable of giving witness to the redemptive power of the Cross of Christ. I pray that by the grace of the Holy Spirit, this time of purification will enable all God's people in Ireland to "maintain and perfect in their lives that holiness which they have received from God" (*Lumen Gentium*, 40).

The fine work and selfless dedication of the great majority of priests and religious in Ireland should not be obscured by the transgressions of some of their brethren. I am certain that the people understand this, and continue to regard their clergy with affection and esteem. Encourage your priests always to seek spiritual renewal and to discover afresh the joy of ministering to their flocks within the great family of the Church.

The prevention of sexual abuse

Our stewardship should also embrace the urgent and long-term issue of the prevention of sexual misconduct in general and of sexual abuse of minors in particular. Notwithstanding the lack of candidates to the priesthood in certain parts of the world, but also to the background of a flourishing of vocations in others, the question of screening of future candidates remains of the essence. The more recent documents of the Congregation for the Clergy on programs of human formation should be studied and implemented thoroughly. To quote from the more recent *Ratio Fundamentalis* (December 8, 2016):

> The greatest attention must be given to the theme of the protection of minors and vulnerable adults, being vigilant that those who seek admission to a Seminary or to a House of Formation, or who are already petitioning to receive Holy Orders, have not been involved in any way with any crime or problematic *behavior* in this area. Formators must ensure that those who have had painful experiences in this area receive special and suitable accompaniment.
>
> Specific lessons, seminars or courses on the protection of minors are to be included in the programs of initial and ongoing formation. Adequate information must be provided in an appropriate fashion, which also gives attention to areas dealing with possible exploitation and violence, such as, for example, the trafficking of minors, child labor, and the sexual abuse of minors or vulnerable adults (n. 202).

A just and balanced understanding of the demands of priestly celibacy and chastity should be underpinned by a profound and healthy formation in human freedom and sound moral doctrine. Candidates for the priesthood and the religious life should nurture and grow in that spiritual fatherhood that should remain the basic motivation for the generous giving of oneself to the faith community in the example of Jesus the Good Shepherd.

The bishop and the religious superior should exercise their spiritual fatherhood vis-à-vis the priests entrusted to their care. This fatherhood is fulfilled through accompaniment with the help of prudent and holy priests. Prevention is better served when protocols are clear and codes of conduct well known. Response to misconduct should be just and even-handed. Outcomes should be clear from the outset. Above all, the Ordinary is responsible in guaranteeing and promoting the personal, physical, mental, and spiritual well-being of his priests. The documents of the magisterium on this issue stress the need for permanent formation and for events and structures of fraternity in the presbyterium.

A good steward will empower his community through information and formation. There are already instances of best practice in a number of countries where whole parish communities have been given specific training in prevention. This valid and positive experience needs to grow in accessibility and extension around the world. Another service to the community is the ready availability of user-friendly access to reporting mechanisms so that a culture of disclosure is not only promoted by words but also encouraged by deed. Protocols for safeguarding should be readily accessible in a clear and direct language. The faith community under our care should know that we mean business. They should come to know us as friends of their safety and that of their children and youth. We will engage them with candor and humility. We will protect them at all cost. We will lay down our lives for the flocks entrusted to us.

Another aspect of the stewardship of prevention is the selection and presentation of candidates for the mission of bishop. Many demand that the process be more open to the input of lay people in the community. We bishops and religious superiors have the sacred duty to help the Holy Father arrive at a proper discernment concerning possible candidates for leadership as bishops. It is a grave sin against the integrity of the episcopal ministry to hide or underestimate facts that may indicate deficits in the lifestyle or spiritual fatherhood of priests subject to a pontifical investigation into their suitability for the office of bishop.

At this point I would like to offer another quote from Pope Benedict XVI's Letter to the People in God in Ireland (March 19, 2010), this time expressly addressed to the bishops:

It cannot be denied that some of you and your predecessors failed, at times grievously, to apply the long-established norms of canon law to the crime of child abuse. Serious mistakes were made in responding to allegations. I recognize how difficult it was to grasp the extent and complexity of the problem, to obtain reliable information and to make the right decisions in the light of conflicting expert advice. Nevertheless, it must be admitted that grave errors of judgment were made and failures of leadership occurred. All this has seriously undermined your credibility and effectiveness. I appreciate the efforts you have made to remedy past mistakes and to guarantee that they do not happen again. Besides fully implementing the norms of canon law in addressing cases of child abuse, continue to cooperate with the civil authorities in their area of competence. Clearly, religious superiors should do likewise. They too have taken part in recent discussions here in Rome with a view to establishing a clear and consistent approach to these matters. It is imperative that the child safety norms of the Church in Ireland be continually revised and updated and that they be applied fully and impartially in conformity with canon law.

Only decisive action carried out with complete honesty and transparency will restore the respect and good will of the Irish people towards the Church to which we have consecrated our lives. This must arise, first and foremost, from your own self-examination, inner purification and spiritual renewal. The Irish people rightly expect you to be men of God, to be holy, to live simply, to pursue personal conversion daily. For them, in the words of Saint Augustine, you are a bishop; yet with them you are called to be a follower of Christ (cf. *Sermon* 340, 1). I therefore exhort you to renew your sense of accountability before God, to grow in solidarity with your people and to deepen your pastoral concern for all the members of your flock. In particular, I ask you to be attentive to the spiritual and moral lives of each one of your priests. Set them an example by your own lives, be close to them, listen to their concerns, offer them encouragement at this difficult time and stir up the flame of their love for Christ and their commitment to the service of their brothers and sisters.

The lay faithful, too, should be encouraged to play their proper part in the life of the Church. See that they are formed in such a way that they can offer an articulate and convincing account of the Gospel in the midst of modern society (cf. 1 Peter 3:15) and cooperate more fully in the Church's life and mission. This in turn will help you once again become credible leaders and witnesses to the redeeming truth of Christ. (n. 11)

Conclusion

As Pope Francis wrote in his "Letter to the People of God" (August 20, 2018):

It is essential that we, as a Church, be able to acknowledge and condemn, with sorrow and shame, the atrocities perpetrated by consecrated persons, clerics, and all those entrusted with the mission of watching over and caring for those most vulnerable. Let us beg forgiveness for our own sins and the sins of others. An awareness of sin helps us to acknowledge the errors, the crimes and the wounds caused in the past and allows us, in the present, to be more open and committed along a journey of renewed conversion.

THE CHURCH IN
A TIME OF CRISIS

*Responsibility of the Bishop: Dealing with
Conflicts and Tensions and Acting Decisively*

CARDINAL RUBÉN SALAZAR GÓMEZ, *Archbishop of Bogotá,
President of the Episcopal Conference of Latin America (CELAM)*

Introduction and context

We are responding today to a very concrete question in the face of the crisis that we are experiencing in the Church. What is the responsibility of the bishop? In order to understand and fulfill this responsibility, it is imperative that we try to define, as far as possible, the nature of the crisis.

A brief analysis of what has happened shows us that it is not only a matter of sexual deviations or pathologies in the abusers, but that there is a deeper root too. This is the distortion of the meaning of ministry, which becomes a means to impose force, to violate the conscience and the bodies of the weakest. This has a name: clericalism.

Moreover, in analyzing the way in which this crisis has generally been responded to, we encounter a mistaken understanding of how to exercise ministry that has led to serious errors of authority, which have increased the severity of the crisis. This has a name: clericalism.

It is this reality that the Holy Father Pope Francis describes in his "Letter to the People of God" in August of last year: "This is clearly seen in a peculiar way of understanding the Church's authority, one common in many communities where sexual abuse and the abuse of power and conscience have occurred. Such is the case with clericalism...To say 'no' to abuse is to say an emphatic 'no' to all forms of clericalism."

Clear words that urge us to go to the root of the problem in order to face it. But it is not easy "to say 'no' to abuse [and thereby] to say an emphatic 'no' to all forms of clericalism," because it is a mentality that has permeated our Church throughout the ages, and we are usually unaware that it underlies our way of conceiving ministry and acting at decisive moments. This observation means that it is necessary to unmask the underlying clericalism and bring about a change of mentality that in more precise terms, is called conversion.

Fundamentally, our responsibility is a meticulous coherence between our words and our actions. A profound revision of the mentality behind our words and actions must occur, so that they correspond to God's will for the Church at this time.

This invitation to conversion is addressed to the whole Church, but first of all to us who are her pastors.

The responsibility of the bishop in light of the office received and his co-responsibility as a member of the episcopal conference under the supreme authority of the Church

1. The bishop's responsibility as pastor

As bishops, our responsibility begins by constantly increasing our awareness that we are nothing on our own. We can do nothing on our own, since it is not we who have chosen the ministry but the Lord who has chosen us (cf. John 15:16–18) to make his salvation present through the action of the Church, without obscuring his presence with the darkness of our counter-witness.

Aware of this task, we have to admit that many times the Church—in the persons of her bishops—did not know (and still, at times, does not know) how to behave as she should in order to face quickly and decisively the crisis caused by abuses. We often proceed like the hirelings who, on seeing the wolf coming, flee and leave the flock unprotected. And we flee in many ways: trying to deny the dimension of the accusations presented to us; not listening to the victims; ignoring the damage caused to the victims of abuse; transferring the accused to other places where they continue to abuse; or trying to reach monetary settlements to buy silence. Acting in this way, we clearly manifest a clerical mentality that leads us to misunderstand the institution of the Church and place it above the suffering of the victims and the demands of justice. This mentality accepts the justifications of the perpetrators over the testimony of those affected. It silences the cry of pain of the victimized so as to avoid the public scandal that an accusation before civil authorities or a trial can provoke. It takes counterproductive measures that ignore the good of the communities and the most vulnerable. Relying exclusively on the advice of lawyers, psychiatrists, and specialists of all kinds, it neglects any deep sense of compassion and mercy. It goes even so far as to lie or distort the facts so as not to confess the horrible reality that presents itself.

This mentality is manifest in the tendency to act as though the Church is not and need not be subject to the power of civil authority, like other citizens, but that we can and must handle all our affairs within the Church governed solely by canon law. This mentality goes so far as to regard the intervention of civil authority as an undue intrusion that, in these times of growing secularism, seems to be inclined to persecute the faith.

We have to recognize this crisis in its full depth, to recognize that the damage is not done by outsiders but that the first enemies are within us, among us bishops and priests and consecrated persons who have not lived up to our vocation. We have to recognize that the enemy is within.

Recognizing and confronting the crisis—overcoming our clerical mentality—also means not minimizing it by asserting that abuses occur on a large scale in other institutions. The fact that abuses occur in other institutions and groups can never justify the occurrence of abuses in the Church, because it contradicts the very essence of the ecclesial community and constitutes a monstrous distortion of the priestly ministry which, by its very nature, must seek the good of souls as its supreme end. There is no possible justification for not denouncing, not unmasking, not courageously and forcefully confronting any abuse that presents itself within our Church.

We also have to recognize that the press and other media and social networks have been very important in helping us to face the crisis rather than sidestep it. The media do a valuable job in this regard, a job that needs to be supported.

As Pope Francis put it in his 2018 Christmas Greetings to the Roman Curia:

> In discussing this scourge, some within the Church take to task certain *communications professionals*, accusing them of ignoring the overwhelming majority of cases of abuse that are not committed by clergy—the statistics speak of more than 95%—and accusing them of intentionally wanting to give the false impression that this evil affects the Catholic Church alone. I myself would like to give heartfelt thanks to those media professionals who were honest and objective and sought to unmask these predators and to make their victims' voices heard. Even if it were to involve a single case of abuse (something itself monstrous), the Church asks that people not be silent but bring it objectively to light, since the greater scandal in this matter is that of cloaking the truth.

There is no doubt that we have already done a great deal to address the crisis of abuse. However, had it not been for the valuable insistence of victims and the pressure exerted by the media, we might not have decided to face this shameful crisis to this degree. The damage caused is so deep, the pain inflicted is so profound, the consequences of the abuses that have taken place in the Church are so immense that we will never be able to say that we have done all that can be done. Our responsibility leads us to work every day so that abuses never happen again in the Church and so that those who do perpetrate abuse receive the punishment they deserve and make appropriate amends.

2. The responsibility of the Bishop as a member of the episcopal college under the supreme authority of the Church

In dealing with this crisis and in the process of conversion that he must undergo in order to face it, the bishop is not alone. His ministry is a collegial ministry. By his episcopal ordination, the bishop becomes part of the college formed by all the successors of the apostles under the guidance and authority of the successor of the apostle Peter. More than ever we must feel called to strengthen our fraternal bonds, to enter into true communal discernment, to act always with the same norms and to support each other in making decisions. Our strength depends, without a doubt, on the profound unity that marks our being and acting.

To help us in this task, the popes have enlightened us with their words, and the various dicasteries of the Roman Curia have issued instructions that show us the road we have to travel. We already know how to proceed, but it seems desirable that a "Code of Conduct" be offered to the bishop which, in harmony with the "Directory for Bishops," clearly shows what the bishop's course of action should be in the context of this crisis. Pope Francis, in his apostolic letter in the form of his motu proprio *As a Loving Mother*, presents us with the requirements for a bishop's action and his removal in the case of proven gross negligence. The "Code of Conduct" will clarify and demand of us the conduct that is proper to the bishop. Its obligatory nature will be a guarantee that we all act in unison and in the right direction, since it gives us clear norms to control our conduct and provides concrete suggestions for the necessary corrective measures. It will be a guide for the Church and society as well, allowing everyone to properly assess the bishop's actions in specific cases and giving us all the confidence that we are doing well. It will also be a concrete way of strengthening the communion that is born of episcopal collegiality.

The ongoing formation of the bishop has been a constant concern of the Church. Changing times pose new challenges to which the bishop must respond. As we face this crisis we need to be in a permanent process of being updated, formed, and instructed, so that our response will always be the right one. This too is an obligatory matter since the world needs to see perfect unity in our response.

Here again, the crisis is a call to a conversion that goes to the depths of our ecclesial life. The present encounter is a clear sign and a real opportunity to grow in this spirit of communion.

3. The responsibility of the bishop toward his priests and consecrated persons

The bishop also has responsibility for the sanctification of priests and consecrated persons. This responsibility encompasses a wide range of activity that begins with the discernment of the vocation of future priests and consecrated persons, continues in initial formation, and persists throughout the entire existence of those who have been called to a life of total dedication to the service of the Church. In the light of the crisis unleashed by reports of sexual abuse by clerics, this responsibility has acquired special dimensions, in which the closeness of the bishop becomes indispensable. The permanent dialogue—as friend, brother, father—that allows the bishop to know his priests and to accompany them in their joys and sorrows, in their achievements and failures, in their difficulties and successes, is the ongoing journey that the bishop must travel in his relationship with his priests.

And what is our responsibility to abusive priests? As bishops, we must fulfill our duty to confront immediately the situation that arises from an accusation. Every accusation must immediately trigger the procedures that are specified both in canon law and in the civil law of each nation, according to the guidelines established by each episcopal conference. The guidelines help us to distinguish between sin subject to divine mercy, ecclesial crime subject to canonical legislation, and civil crime subject to the corresponding civil legislation. These are fields that should not be confused and that, when properly distinguished and separated, allow us to act with full justice. Today it is clear to us that any negligence on our part can lead to canonical penalties, including removal from ministry, and civil penalties that can even lead to imprisonment for concealment or complicity.

Throughout the canonical process, it is essential that the accused be heard. The bishop's gracious closeness is a first step toward the recovery of the offender. Conscientiously following the guidelines drawn by the episcopal conference allows the bishop to demonstrate for his diocese the route that will be followed in the various cases of accusations of abuse by a cleric. The special care that is taken in this implementation will determine to a large extent whether the case is treated with full justice. But it is not enough to prosecute and convict the accused when guilt is established; it is also necessary to provide for his treatment so that there is no relapse.

How justice is implemented concretely in the different processes that deal with abusive clerics is one of the most important factors in overcoming the crisis with regard to the health of priests, since one often hears people say, "Where are the rights of priests?" The fact that there are guilty priests and consecrated persons cannot, under any circumstances, justify unfair treatment of the offenders. In the preliminary investigations, in both canonical and civil processes, safeguarding the inalienable rights of the possible perpetrators has been and must always be a concern. Furthermore, it has often been the fear of violating these rights that has led to actions that were later described as cover-up and complicity. However, we must be clear that the rights of the perpetrators—for example, to their good reputation, to the exercise of their ministry, to continue leading a normal life within society—can never take precedence over the rights of the victims, of the weakest, of the most vulnerable.

4. The bishop's responsibility to the faithful, holy people of God

How have Catholics reacted to the scandal of abuses by clergy and consecrated persons? There is no unequivocal answer to that, but once again it has been noted that for the vast majority of both Catholics and non-Catholics, the Church is identified with her priests and consecrated persons. It is the Church that is held responsible for what has happened. This reality should motivate us to grow ever closer to the People of God who are called to grow each day in their awareness of belonging to the Church and of feeling co-responsible for her.

It is in the context of being close to God's people that we must understand our approach to the victims of abuse. And our first duty is to listen to them. One of the first sins committed at the beginning of the crisis was precisely not having listened with open hearts to those who charged that they had been abused by clerics.

Listening to the victims begins by not minimizing the pain and damage that were caused. In many cases it was thought that the only motive behind the accusations was to seek financial compensation. "The only thing they are looking for is money" was the recurrent phrase. There is no doubt that accusations are sometimes orchestrated. There is also no doubt that on many occasions, attempts have been made to reduce the redress to the victims in terms of monetary compensation without taking into account the true scope of that compensation. And there is no doubt that on many occasions, we have also given in to the temptation to try to fix unsustainable situations with money in order to silence a probable scandal. This harmful reality must not stop us, however, from becoming aware of our serious and grave responsibility for the redress and compensation of victims. Money can never repair the damage caused, but it becomes necessary in many cases so that the victims can receive the psychotherapeutic treatments they need, which are generally very expensive. Some victims have been unable to recover from the damage caused; they cannot work and need economic support to survive. For some the pecuniary recognition becomes part of acknowledging the damage caused. It is clear that we are obliged to offer them all the necessary means—spiritual, psychological, psychiatric, social—for their recovery. The responsibility of the bishop is very broad and covers many fields, but it is always inescapable.

Conclusion

In his address to the American cardinals on April 23, 2002, St. John Paul II provided the essential direction that all our efforts must follow to overcome the current crisis: "So much pain, so much sorrow must lead to a holier priesthood, a holier episcopate, and a holier Church." With the Lord's help and with our docility to his grace, this crisis will lead to a profound renewal of the whole Church, with holier bishops, more aware of their mission as pastors and fathers of the flock; with holier priests and consecrated persons, more dedicated to exemplary service to God's people; with a holier People of God, more aware of their co-responsibility to build permanently a Church of communion and participation, where everyone, especially children and adolescents, always finds a safe place that promotes their human growth and their living of the faith. In this way we will contribute to eradicating the culture of abuse in the world in which we live.

TESTIMONIAL

OF A VICTIM

OF SEXUAL ABUSE

THE BRIDGE THAT MADE THE DIFFERENCE

Out came a boy,
Into a world that was new;
A challenge it was
Like for any newborn.
Who ever thought that this world
Brought him surprises and dangers unsought!

The quest for a good Catholic formation
Made him depart
From an environment—happy and whole;
A just cause it was,
And so with grief he bade farewell
To all that he knew:
Parents, siblings, love, care,
Protection and all.

As young as five,
To a world unknown,
He entered full of innocence and fears
into halls that were new.
He missed home and
Searched here for friends
And guardians to be his parents.
Fatal was this replacement
Because he was young
and their desires were strange.
Stripped of his innocence
Again and again,
Left to fend for himself
In this adult world,

He abandoned hope
And became a recluse.
With the passing of years
It shred him in pieces.
But he could tell no one,
For fear of disgrace and shame.

From learning more of "Christian values"
He withdrew from the world
To the safety of being quiet, hidden within;
For secrecy was the only way out.

Many times did he question:
What was this world?
It made no sense nor gave him hope.
Once he contemplated over a bridge,
And asked himself, "How would his way down change,
Change the order of things?"
Never was there an answer.

Who will ever know
What he went through?
Who will ever ask?
Who will ever take the responsibility
For this life that seemed lost?

Not a thing in his life
Was left untouched.
All of it was marred.
Was God ever there?
For He would be the only one
Who knows it all.

The bridge that he contemplated

Did show him a way,
a way that was different
That came to fruition, when
He strangely heard in his noisy, troubled heart
A voice that called for a change to be brought.
A journey he began.
To fulfill what the voice said.
A journey of forgiveness,
A journey of reconciliation
A journey that accepted the life that was
A life full of hurt, sorrow and despair.

That new way down the bridge
Was long and difficult.
It touched his very essence of life.
But, a way there was, a different one;
A way that heals, a healing that takes time.
It softened his hardened heart
And transformed the life he lived.
It broke the shell he lived in, to walk free
And tell the world, "There is a way."
That's his story.

But now, who will take the responsibility
Of lives that are broken?
There is a way!
There is a chance!
There is hope!
There is life!
Bring back what is lost!
Show that you care!
For all that you do
Will save the many silent cries
That wait for a saving day.

FEBRUARY 22, 2019

Accountability

PRESENTATIONS

THE NECESSITY OF ACCOUNTABILITY

in a Collegial and Synodal Church

CARDINAL OSWALD GRACIAS, *Archbishop of Bombay,*
President of the Episcopal Conference of India

Sexual abuse in the Catholic Church and the subsequent failure to address it in an open, accountable, and effective way has caused a multifaceted crisis that has gripped and wounded the Church, not to speak of those who have been abused. Although the experience of abuse seems dramatically present in certain parts of the world, it is not a limited phenomenon. Indeed, the entire Church must take an honest look, undertake rigorous discernment, and then act decisively to prevent abuse from occurring in the future and to do whatever possible to foster healing for victims.

The importance and universal scope of this challenge has prompted Pope Francis to summon us to this meeting, underscoring his commitment and the Church's commitment to addressing this crisis. Even more, by inviting the presidents of national conferences of bishops, he is signaling how the Church must address this crisis. For him and for those of us gathered with him, it will be the path of collegiality and synodality. That way of being the Church will then—with God's help—shape and define how the whole Church at the regional, national, local-diocesan, and even parochial levels will take up the task of addressing sexual abuse in the Church.

Thus, synodality can truly be lived by incorporating all decisions and the resulting measures at all these different levels on a binding basis. This includes the involvement of lay people, both men and women. In doing so, we should remain honest, and ask ourselves: do we really want this? What are we actually doing toward this? Are we only undertaking alibi measures for a synodal church, and in reality actually wish to remain among ourselves as bishops—in "our" conferences, in "our" commissions, in "our" meetings, in which non-bishops and non-clergy only play an insignificant role? Now is not the time and place to go into detail, but if we do not only speak of a synodal church but also want to live it, then we must also learn to practice other forms of management, and learn how we can conduct synodical processes. If we do not do all of this, then the talk of synodality in the context of the topic of abuse only serves to conceal inconsistent behavior, i.e., in the critical and difficult field of abuse, deflecting responsibility onto lay people (men and women), but otherwise denying them the opportunity to take responsibility.

Permit me to frame this in a personal perspective. No bishop should say to himself, "I face these problems and challenges alone." Because we belong to the college of bishops in union with the Holy Father, we all share accountability and responsibility. Collegiality is an essential context for addressing wounds of abuse inflicted on victims and on the Church at large. We bishops need to return to the teaching of the Second Vatican Council often, in order to find ourselves in the larger mission and ministry of the Church. Consider these words from *Lumen Gentium*: "The individual bishops, who are placed in charge of particular churches, exercise their pastoral government over the portion of the People of God committed to their care...But each of them, as a member of the episcopal college and legitimate successor of the apostles, is obliged by Christ's institution and command to be solicitous for the whole Church" (n. 23).

The point is clear. No bishop may say to himself, "This problem of abuse in the Church does not concern me, because things are different in my part of the world." We are each responsible for the whole church. We hold accountability and responsibility together. We extend our concern beyond our local Church to embrace all the churches with which we are in communion.

As we take up our collegial and collective sense of accountability and responsibility, we will inevitably encounter a certain dialectic. For our collegiality does indeed express the variety and universality of the People of God, but also the unity of the flock of Christ. There is, in other words, an abiding need to appreciate the great diversity in the lived experience of the churches spread throughout the world because of their history, culture, and customs. At the same time, we must also appreciate and foster our unity, our single mission and purpose, which is to be "like a sacrament or as a sign and instrument both of a very closely knit union with God and of the unity of the whole human race" (*Lumen Gentium*, n. 1). In our church, we urgently need further development of intercultural competences, which ultimately must prove their worth by successful intercultural communication, and corresponding well-founded decision-making.

Practically, this means that as we address the scourge of sexual abuse together, that is, collegially, we must do so with a singular and unified vision as well as with the flexibility and adaptiveness that stems from the diversity of people and situations in our universal care.

In this context, we must also ask ourselves fundamentally whether we adequately live what is meant by the concepts of collegiality and synodality. Collegiality and synodality must not only remain theoretical concepts, which are extensively described but not put into practice. In this regard, I still see plenty of scope for further developments. Perhaps we can make progress, if we can clarify the following points.

1. It cannot be disregarded that dealing with the topic of abuse in the right way has been difficult for us in the church, for various reasons. We as bishops also bear responsibility for this. For me, this raises the question: Do we really engage in an open conversation and point out honestly to our brother bishops or priests when we notice problematic behavior in them? We should cultivate a culture of *correctio fraterna*, which enables this without offending each other, and at the same time recognize criticism from a brother as an opportunity to better fulfill our tasks.

2. Closely related to this point is willingness to personally admit mistakes to each other, and to ask for help, without feeling the need to maintain the pretense of own perfection. Do we really have the kind of fraternal relationship, where in such cases we don't have to worry about damaging ourselves, simply because we show weakness?

3. For a bishop, the relationship with the Holy Father is of constitutive significance. Every bishop is obliged to directly obey and follow the

Holy Father. We should ask ourselves honestly, whether on this basis we don't sometimes think that our relationship with the other bishops is not so important, especially if the brothers have a different opinion, and/or if they feel the need to correct us. Do we perhaps ignore the input from our brothers, because ultimately only the pope can give us orders in any case, and therefore collegiality is easy to ignore, or in such cases has no relevant clout?

4. If in such contexts we ourselves always refer back to Rome, we shouldn't wonder if a certain Roman centralism does not sufficiently take into account the diversity in our brotherhood, and our local church competencies and our skills as responsible shepherds of our local churches are not appropriately used, and thereby the practically lived collegiality suffers. If we want to and must revitalize our collegiality, then we also need a discussion between the Roman Curia and our bishops' conferences. We can always only take responsibility for something insofar as we are allowed to do so, and the more responsibility we are granted, the better we can serve our own flock.

5. Whether it is the relationship between us local bishops and Rome, or the relationship of the bishops among themselves, one important aspect should be clear. Collegiality can only be lived and practiced on the basis of communication. We must ask ourselves whether we really utilize all forms of modern, regular, and sustainable communication, or whether we are still lagging behind. In all honesty, I do believe that we could improve in this regard, for example both in terms of speed of information exchange, as well as in the forms of participation for opinion formation, and the forms of discussion.

I am firmly convinced that there are no real alternatives to collegiality and synodality in our interaction. But before I note some practical consequences for addressing sexual abuse in the Church from a collegial perspective, permit me to summarize the challenge that we face together.

The challenge of sexual abuse in the Church

The sexual abuse of minors and vulnerable adults in the Church reveals a complex web of interconnected factors, including psychopathology, sinful moral decisions, social environments that enable abuse to happen, and often inadequate or plainly harmful institutional and pastoral responses, or a lack of response. The abuse perpetrated by clerics (bishops, priests, deacons) and others serving in the Church (e.g., teachers, catechists, coaches) results in incalculable damage that is both direct and indirect. Most important, abuse inflicts damage on the survivors. This direct damage can be physical. Inevitably, it is psychological with all the long-term consequences of any serious emotional trauma related to a profound betrayal of trust. Very often, it is a form of direct spiritual damage that shakes faith and severely disrupts the spiritual journey of those who suffer abuse, sometimes spiraling them into despair.

The indirect damage of abuse often results from a failed or inadequate institutional response to the sexual abuse. Included in that kind of indirect and damaging response might be: failure to listen to victims or to take their claims seriously, not extending care and support to victims and their families, giving priority to protecting institutional and financial concerns (for example, by "hiding" abuse and abusers) over and above the care of victims, failing to withdraw abusers from situations that would enable them to abuse other victims, and not offering programs of formation and screening for those who work with children and vulnerable adults. As serious as the direct abuse of children and vulnerable adults is, the indirect damage inflicted by those with directive responsibility within the Church can be worse by re-victimizing those who have already suffered abuse.

Addressing sexual abuse in the Church represents a complex and multifaceted challenge, perhaps unprecedented in the Church's history because of today's communications and global connections. This makes collegiality even more decisive in our current situation. But how ought a collegial Church respond to that challenge? If we use the elements of collegiality as a lens for viewing and addressing the crisis, we can perhaps begin to make some progress. Surely, addressing the crisis does not mean a quick or definitive resolution. We will need to begin courageously and persevere resolutely on the road together.

For now, I want to indicate three themes that I consider especially important for our reflection: justice, healing, and pilgrimage.

Justice

The sexual abuse of others, most especially minors, is rooted in an unjust sense of entitlement: "I can claim this person for my use and abuse." Although sexual abuse is many things, such as a breach of trust and a betrayal of confidence, it is at root an act of grave injustice. Victim-survivors speak of their sense of being unjustly violated. A fundamental task that belongs to all of us individually and collegially is to restore justice to those who have been violated. There are multiple levels at work in this process of restoration. Of course, we must stand for and promote God's justice and implement the standards of justice that belong to our Church community. Ecclesiastical law and process must be implemented fairly and effectively. There is, however, more to the story.

The sexual abuse of minors and other vulnerable people not only breaks divine and ecclesiastical law, it is also public criminal behavior. The Church does not only live in an isolated world of its own making. The Church lives in the world and with the world. Those who are guilty of criminal behavior are justly accountable to civil authority for that behavior. Although the Church is not an agent of the state, the Church recognizes the legitimate authority of civil law and the state. Therefore, the Church cooperates with civil authorities in these matters to bring justice to survivors and to the civil order.

Complications ensue when there are antagonistic relations between the Church and the state or, even more dramatically, when the state persecutes or stands ready to persecute the Church. These kinds of circumstances underscore the importance of collegiality. Only in a network of strong relationships among the bishops and the local Churches working together can the Church navigate the turbulent waters of Church-state conflict and, at the same time, appropriately address the crime of sexual abuse. There is a double need that only collegiality can address: the need for shared wisdom and the need for supportive encouragement.

Healing

In addition to standing for justice, a collegial Church stands for healing. Certainly, that healing must reach out to the victims of abuse. It must also extend to others who are affected including the communities whose trust was betrayed or severely tested.

For effective healing to happen, there must be clear, transparent, and consistent communication from a collegial Church to victims, members of the Church, and society at large. In that communication, the Church offers several messages.

1. The first message, directed especially to victims, is a respectful outreach and an honest acknowledgment of their pain and hurt. Although this would seem to be obvious, it has not always been communicated. Ignoring or minimizing what victims have experienced only exacerbates their pain and delays their healing. Within a collegial Church, we can summon each other to attentiveness and compassion that enable us to make this outreach and acknowledgment.

2. The second message must be an offer to heal. There are many paths to healing, from professional counseling to support groups of peers and other means as well. In a collegial Church, we can exercise our imagination and develop these various paths of healing that we can, in turn, communicate to those who are hurting.

3. A third important message is to identify and implement measure to protect young and vulnerable people from future abuse. Again, it takes a collective wisdom and a shared imagination to develop the ways of protecting young people and avoiding the tragedy of abuse. That can happen in a collegial Church that assumes responsibility for the future.

4. A fourth and final message is directed to society at large. Our Holy Father has wisely and correctly said that abuse is a human problem. It is not, of course, limited to the Church. In fact, it is a pervasive and

sad reality across all sectors of life. Out of this particularly challenging moment in the life of the Church, we—again in a collegial context—can draw on and develop resources which can be of great service to a larger world. The grace of this moment can actually be our ability to serve a great need in the world from our experience in the Church.

Pilgrimage

As we face the tragedy of sexual abuse in the Church, as we encounter the suffering of victims, we are never more conscious of our status as the pilgrim People of God. We know that we have not yet arrived at our destination. We are aware that our journey has not been along a straight path. The Second Vatican Council captured this so well in *Lumen Gentium*:

> Already the final age of the world has come upon us and the renovation of the world is irrevocably decreed and is already anticipated in some kind of a real way; for the Church already on this earth is signed with a sanctity which is real although imperfect. However, until there shall be new heavens and a new earth in which justice dwells, the pilgrim Church in her sacraments and institutions, which pertain to this present time, has the appearance of this world which is passing and she herself dwells among creatures who groan and travail in pain until now and await the revelation of the sons of God. (n. 48)

To be the pilgrim People of God does not simply mean that we have a certain unfinished *status*, although that is indeed the case. To be the pilgrim People of God means that we are a community that is called to continuous repentance and continuous discernment. We must repent—and do so together, collegially—because along the way we have failed. We need to seek pardon. We must also be in a process of continuous discernment. In other words, together or collegially, we need to watch, wait, observe, and discover the direction that God is giving us in the circumstances of our lives. There is more ahead of us. As the abuse crisis has unfolded, we have come to know that there is no easy or quick solution. We are summoned to move forward step by step and together. That requires discernment.

Conclusion

Recently, in a very different context, the bishops of the Congo came together and acted collegially. With great courage and determination, they addressed the social and political challenges of their nation. They did so, not one by one but rather together, collegially. In their mutual and shared support, they brought forth a witness to what lived collegiality can mean and how effective it can be.

As we reflect on the abuse crisis which has afflicted the Church, we do well to draw from their example and recognize the power of collegiality in addressing the most challenging issues that face us.

In order for us to move forward with a clear sense of accountability and responsibility in a context of collegiality, there are—as I see it—at least four requisites, which I offer for your consideration.

To take up collegiality in order to address our accountability and responsibility, we must:

1. claim, or better reclaim, our identity in the apostolic college united with Peter's successor, and we must do so with humility and openness;
2. summon courage and fortitude, because the path ahead is not mapped out with great detail and clear-cut precision;
3. embrace the path of practical discernment, because we want to fulfill what God wants of us in the concrete circumstances of our lives;
4. be willing to pay the price of following God's will in uncertain and painful circumstances.

If we do these things, we will be able to move forward collegially on a path of accountability and responsibility. But notice that all these actions are not simply our actions; they are the work of the Holy Spirit: to claim identity or to know who we are, to live with courage and fortitude, to be discerning, and to be generous in service. So, let the last word be *Veni, Sancte Spiritus, veni.*

SYNODALITY:
JOINTLY RESPONSIBLE

CARDINAL BLASE CUPICH,
Archbishop of Chicago

Introduction: from collegiality to synodality

From what we just heard from Cardinal Gracias, we are to understand our gathering in these days as an exercise in collegiality. We are here, as the universal episcopate in affective and substantive union with the successor of Peter, to discern through spirited dialogue where our ministry as successors of the apostles calls us to confront effectively the scandal of clergy sexual abuse that has wounded so many little ones.

While we share a unique responsibility in this regard as the college of bishops, it is also imperative that we consider the challenge we face in the light of synodality, especially as we explore with the entire Church the structural, legal and institutional aspects of accountability. For synodality represents the participation of all the baptized at every level—in parishes, dioceses, national and regional ecclesial bodies—in a discernment and reform that penetrates throughout the Church. It is precisely such a penetrating discernment, so vital to the Church in this moment, that will give rise to the elements of truth, penitence, and renewal of cultures that are essential to fulfilling the mandate of protecting the young within the Church and in turn within the larger society. A process that merely changes policies, even if it is the fruit of the finest acts of collegiality, is not enough. It is the conversion of men and women throughout the entire Church —parents and priests, catechists and religious, parish leaders and bishops—and the conversion of ecclesial cultures on every continent that we must seek. Only a synodal vision, rooted in discernment, conversion, and reform at every level can bring to the Church the comprehensive action in the defense of the most vulnerable in our midst to which God's grace is calling us.

A sacred bond

With that in mind, I want to begin with a story. Sixty years ago, this past December, a fire raged through Our Lady of the Angels Catholic elementary school in Chicago, taking the lives of ninety-two children and three religious sisters. To mark that sad anniversary, I presided at a Memorial Mass, attended by many of the former students who survived the fire and family members of those who had died. One of the persons I greeted before the Mass was a ninety-five-year-old mother of one of the children who died in the fire. She was an Italian immigrant, who told me in her native language, but also by the pitiful look in her tearful eyes, that the sting of her loss was still as sharp as the day her nine-year-old daughter perished. She showed me the holy card with her daughter's picture. She clutched it in her hand as something very precious. She had kept this *santino* for six decades since the day of her little girl's funeral.

This moving story of a grieving mother, a modern-day Pietà, who lost her child many years ago puts us in touch on a profoundly human level with the sacred bond a parent has with a child. I believe that this sacred space of family life must be the point of reference and where we find our motivation as we commit ourselves in these days to build a culture of accountability with proper structures to radically alter our approach to child safeguarding. Sadly, many of our people, not just those abused or parents of the abused, but the faithful at large are wondering if we the leaders of the Church fully understand this reality, particularly when they see little care given to abused children, or even worse, when it is covered up to protect the abuser or the institution. They are asking themselves, "If church leaders could act with so little care in giving pastoral attention in such obvious cases of a child being sexually molested, does that not reveal how detached they are from us as parents who treasure our children as the light of our lives? Can we really expect our leaders to care about us and our children in the ordinary circumstances of life, if they responded so callously in cases that would alarm any reasonable person?" This is the source of the growing mistrust in our leadership, not to mention the outrage of our people.

My point is simple. None of the structural elements we enact as a synodal Church, important as they are, can guide us forward faithfully in Christ unless we anchor all our deliberations in the piercing pain of those who have been abused and of the families who have suffered with them. The Church must become like the grieving mother, whom I encountered in Chicago; the Church must truly be Pietà, broken in suffering, consoling in enveloping love, constant in pointing to the divine tenderness of God amidst the pangs of desolation in those who have been crushed by clergy abuse.

Four synodal principles to focus structural legal and institutional reform

For a Church seeking to be a loving mother in the face of clergy sexual abuse, four orientations, rooted in synodality, must shape every structural, legal, and institutional reform designed to meet the enormous challenge that the reality of sexual abuse by clergy represents at this moment.

1. Radical listening

The first orientation is a perpetual stance of radical listening to comprehend the deadening experience of those who have been sexually abused by clergy. This is how we are to understand the Holy Father's request that we prepare for this meeting by entering personally into the experiences of survivors by visiting with them. The Church as a loving mother must continually open herself to the heartbreaking reality of children whose wounds will never heal. Such a stance of listening calls us to cast aside the institutional distance and relational blinders that insulate us from coming face to face with the raw destruction of the lives of children and vulnerable people that clergy sexual abuse brings. Our listening cannot be passive, waiting for those who have been abused to find a way to us. Rather, our listening must be active, searching out those who have been wounded, and seeking to minister to them. Our listening must be willing to accept challenge, and confrontation, and even condemnation for the Church's past and present failures to keep safe the most precious of the Lord's flock. Our listening must be vigilant, understanding that only by inquiry and perseverance and action in the face of signs of sexual abuse can we fulfill God's mandate. Finally, our listening must bring with it the willingness to con-

front the past grave and callous errors of some bishops and religious superiors in addressing cases of clergy sexual abuse, and the discernment to
understand how to establish just accountability for these massive failures.

2. Lay witness

The second foundation that must orient every structural reform to
address clergy sexual abuse in a synodal Church is the affirmation that
every member of the Church has an essential role in helping the Church
to eliminate the horrific reality of clergy sexual abuse. In large part it is
the witness of the laity, especially mothers and fathers with great love for
the Church, who have pointed out movingly and forcefully how gravely
incompatible the commission, cover-up, and toleration of clergy sexual
abuse is with the very meaning and essence of the Church. This witness of
faith and justice by the laity represents not a confrontational challenge to
the Church, but an ongoing and grace-filled testimony of faith and action
that is essential for the pilgrim People of God to fulfill its salvific mission
at this moment in history. Mothers and fathers have called us to account,
for they simply cannot comprehend how we as bishops and religious superiors have often been blinded to the scope and damage of sexual abuse of
minors. They are witnessing to dual realities that must be pursued in our
church today: an unceasing effort to eradicate clergy sexual abuse in the
Church and a rejection of the clerical culture that so often bred that abuse.

True synodality in the Church calls us to see this broad lay witness
as empowering and accelerating the mission for which we have come
together from every nation in pursuit of the safety of God's children. We
must unswervingly incorporate broad lay participation into every effort
to identify and construct structures of accountability for the prevention of
clergy sexual abuse. For the history of the past decades demonstrates that
the unique and graced perspective of lay men and women, mothers and
fathers, informs our Church in so profound a manner on this tragedy that
any pathway forward that excludes or diminishes it will inevitably deform
the Church and dishonor our God.

3. Collegiality

The third orientation for our work of reform and renewal was noted by Cardinal Gracias this morning: the stance of sustained collegiality that is necessary for any genuine accountability regarding clergy sexual abuse. I know that at times the issue of sexual abuse can leave each of us feeling isolated or defensive in understanding how we should move forward. It is precisely for that reason that our efforts toward structural and legal reform in the Church must be rooted in a profoundly collegial vision. We are gathered here in this historic moment because the Holy Father has powerfully crystallized the drive for reform in a way that positions the Church to meet its responsibilities in protecting the young and to exercise its role as Pietà in a world that knows all too tragically the reality of sexual abuse.

An approach that is synodal and collegial is marked by the reciprocal exchange of mutual knowledge, in the Roman Curia, episcopal conferences, and metropolitans, and among each of them for the purpose of discernment. Rather than operating in isolation, we need to communicate with one another in a spirit of trust, recognizing all the while that we are being faithful to the wishes of Christ, who has united us as successors of the apostles in the gift of the same Spirit. This past year has taught us that the systematic failures in holding clerics of all rank responsible are due in large measure to flaws in the way we interact and communicate with each other in the college of bishops in union with the successor of Peter. But they also reveal in too many cases an inadequate understanding and implementation of key theological realities such as the relationship between the pope and the bishops, bishops among themselves, bishops and religious superiors, bishops with their people, and the role of bishops' conferences.

Pope Francis reminded us in an address to the Congregation of Bishops: "No one can manage everything; each one, with humility and honesty, lays his own badge in a mosaic that belongs to God."[1] In other words, accountability within the college of bishops, marked by synodality, can be shaped in a way that becomes a grounded network of guidance,

---

1   Pope Francis, "Address to the Congregation of Bishops," February 27, 2014.

grace, and support that does not leave the individual leader alone in difficult situations or rely on the false impression that the Holy See must come up with all the answers.

4. Accountability

The final orienting principle essential to effective structures of accountability for clergy sexual abuse is the call to accompaniment. If the Church is truly to embrace victims/survivors of clerical abuse in her arms as a loving mother, then every structure of accountability must include outreach and accompaniment that is truly compassionate. Accompaniment entails genuinely attempting to understand the experience and spiritual journey of the other. Thus, the structures of reporting, investigation, and the evaluation of claims of abuse must always be designed and evaluated with an understanding of what survivors undergo as they approach the Church and seek justice. Each instance of a survivor approaching the Church, whether he or she is seeking solace or justice, retribution or peace, is an invitation for the Church to genuinely be Pietà, marked with tenderness and empathy.

Such structures of accountability must also be just and sure, producing sanctions to protect the vulnerable when the accused is guilty and declarations of innocence when the accused is blameless. The call of the Church to accompany victims demands a mindset that categorically rejects cover-ups or the counsel to distance ourselves from survivors of abuse for legal reasons or out of a fear of scandal that blocks true accompaniment with those who have been victimized. It also demands that we erect structures and legal provisions that manifestly enshrine the duty to protect the young and the vulnerable as their first and overarching principle. Perhaps most importantly, the call to accompaniment demands that bishops and religious superiors reject a clerical worldview that sees charges of clergy sexual abuse cast against a backdrop of status and immunities for those in the clerical state. Authentic Christ-like accompaniment sees all as equal in the Lord, and structures rooted in accompaniment make all feel and appear equal in the Lord.

These four synodal principals of listening, lay witness, collegiality, and accompaniment are constitutive of the Holy Father's call to us to prepare for and open our hearts to the immensity and the importance of the task we undertake in these days.

Institutional and legal structures for accountability: a framework

The task before us is to focus these principles upon the design of specific institutional and legal structures for the purpose of creating genuine accountability in cases related to the misconduct of bishops and religious superiors, and their mishandling of cases of child abuse. But, this will demand that we call each other to an evangelical accountability, anchored in justice and in the sensitivity which Jesus showed when "deeply moved by the sufferings of others…[and] how much his heart was open to others."[2] With all of that in mind, we now turn to what the specific application of accountability through institutional and legal structures might look like in cases involving the misconduct of bishops and their mishandling of cases of child abuse.

As a Loving Mother

We already, of course, have a guide in the apostolic letter *As a Loving Mother*,[3] which sets forth procedures that address, among other things, bishops who mishandle abuse cases. Briefly stated, a bishop, eparch, or major superior of religious institutes and societies of apostolic life of pontifical right can be removed if his lack of diligence in this regard is grave, even if there is no serious, intentional fault on his part. The competent Rome congregation opens an inquiry in accord with Church law to determine if there is foundational proof. The accused will be informed and given the possibility of defending himself. Other bishops or eparchs of the respective bishops' conference or synod may be consulted before the congregation takes a decision. If removal is the judgment, it is submitted

---

2 Pope Francis, *Amoris Laetitia* (March 19, 2016), n. 144.

3 Pope Francis, *As a Loving Mother* (June 4, 2016).

to the Holy Father for approval, and if upheld, the congregation can issue a decree or ask the bishop to resign within fifteen days. Otherwise, the congregation can proceed with removal.[4] We need to read and re-read this letter.

The task ahead

What remains to be enacted are clear procedures in cases which for "grave reasons" could justify the removal from office of a bishop, eparch, or religious superior as defined in the motu proprio *Sacramentorum Sanctitatis Tutela*[5] and the motu proprio *As a Loving Mother*.

What I offer here are relevant factors that must be considered as each episcopal conference adopts procedures that equips a synodal church to hold bishops involved in misconduct and mishandling accountable. My aim is to offer a framework that is in keeping with our ecclesiological and canonical traditions in order to spark conversation among ourselves, knowing that there are differences in culture, civil and canonical laws, and other factors that need to be considered, and yet aware of the urgency that we take decisive action without delay.

I will group my remarks under three headings: 1.) Setting Standards for Investigation of Bishops; 2.) Reporting Allegations; and 3.) Concrete Procedural Steps.

1. Setting standards

As episcopal conferences, provinces, or dioceses collegially establish standards for conducting the investigations of bishops, they should involve and consult lay experts in accord with canon law and explore the use of the Metropolitan, given his traditional role in ordering ecclesial life. All of this should be done without prejudice to the authority of the Holy See.

---

4   In addition, presently, an effort is underway to guarantee that the procedures are standardized among the congregations, but the law is already applicable and in force, as is evidenced in recent cases.

5   Cf. Norms on *delicta graviora*, arts. 1-6.

2. Reporting allegations

All mechanisms for reporting allegations of abuse or mishandling of abuse cases against a bishop should be transparent and well known to the faithful. Attention should be given to establishing independent reporting mechanisms in the form of a dedicated telephone line and/or web portal service to receive and transmit the allegations directly to the Apostolic Nuncio, the Metropolitan[6] of the accused bishop, or as needed his alternate and any lay experts provided for in norms established by the episcopal conferences. The involvement of lay experts to assist from this point forward is for the good of the process and the value of transparency. Other requirements and procedures for reporting to appropriate ecclesiastical authorities by members of the clergy with knowledge of a bishop's misconduct should also be established.

3. Concrete procedural steps

In my view, it will be useful to adopt clear procedural steps that are both rooted in the traditions and structures of the Church and at the same time fulfill modern needs to identify and investigate potentially illicit conduct by bishops. While universal laws may be issued by the Holy See with regard to this issue—and the motu proprio *As a Loving Mother* is the perfect example—episcopal conferences, after appropriate consultations, should consider adopting special norms to address the particular needs of each Conference. I believe our Church is best served if the following principles find their way into any proposed legislation in this area:

---

6   Alternatives to the Metropolitan should be established if he is the accused or if the Metropolitan See is vacant. The alternate could be the nearest Metropolitan within the same episcopal conference, or one from a list created *a priori* by each episcopal conference. Otherwise, the allegation could be forwarded to the senior suffragan bishop of the Province, who assumes the role of the Metropolitan in these cases. In the case of an allegation against a bishop of an Eastern Catholic Church, it could be forwarded to the Patriarch, the Major Archbishop, or the Metropolitan of the Metropolitan Churches *sui iuris*, depending on the structure of the Eastern Catholic Church, unless another provision is made by the Holy See.

a) Victims and their families, as well as persons who report the allegation, need to be treated with dignity and respect and should receive appropriate pastoral care. Efforts should be made to ensure that victims receive psychological counseling and other support, which I believe should be funded by the diocese of the accused bishop.

b) The reporting of an offense should not by impeded by the official secret or confidentiality rules.

c) No person should be discriminated against or retaliated against based upon the reporting of an allegation against a bishop to ecclesiastical authorities.

d) Due attention should be given to including competent lay women and men with expertise in the process from beginning to end, out of respect for the principles of accountability and transparency that I have noted above.[7]

e) Whenever warranted, and at any time during the investigation, the Metropolitan should be able to recommend to the competent Roman congregation that appropriate precautionary measures, including temporary and public withdrawal of the accused from his office, be adopted.

f) If the allegation has even the semblance of truth, which the Metropolitan should be free to determine with the help of lay experts, the Metropolitan can request from the Holy See authorization to investigate. The exact nature of the investigation—whether penal or administrative—would depend on the allegations.[8] This request is

---

7   It is recognized that lay professionals with specialized knowledge may be duly authorized to carry out an investigation, but all investigations must remain under the appropriate ecclesiastical authority. See, e.g., CIC, c. 274 §1 ("Only clerics can obtain offices for whose exercise the power of orders or the power of ecclesiastical governance is required."); see also CIC, cc. 1405, 1717. This, however, does not impede the rights and duties of the laity in making their opinion known to the pastors and the rest of the Christian faithful on matters which concern the good of the Church (see CIC, c. 212 §3).

8   This would not always be a *penal* investigation under canon law, because *As a Loving Mother* also covers non-penal misconduct (such as negligence).

to be forwarded without delay and the congregation should respond without delay.

g) After the Metropolitan receives authorization, he should gather all relevant information expeditiously in collaboration with lay experts to ensure the professional and rapid execution of the investigation and conclude the investigation promptly.

h) Any investigation should be conducted with due respect for the privacy and good name of all persons involved. This does not preclude, however, episcopal conferences adopting norms for informing the faithful of the allegation against the bishop at any stage of the process. At the same time, it is important that the accused be accorded the presumption of innocence during the investigation.[9]

i) Upon completion of the investigation, the Metropolitan would forward the *acta*, including all information gathered with the help of lay experts, along with his *votum*, if requested, to the Holy See.

j) A common fund may be established at the national, regional, or provincial level to cover the costs of the investigations of bishops,[10] with due regard to the norms of canon law for its administration.[11]

k) The competence of the Metropolitan would normally cease once the investigation is completed,[12] but it could be extended to assure continuing pastoral care or for other specific reasons. The processing of the case of a bishop proceeds from this point according to the norms of universal law.[13] In accordance with canon law, the Holy See will either take the case of a bishop to itself for purposes

---

9   All appropriate steps shall be taken to protect the exercise of the rights afforded under canon law. CIC, c. 221; see also *As a Loving Mother*, 2 §2.

10   Cf. CIC, c. 1274 §§3-5.

11   CIC, c. 1275. Lay people can be selected to administer funds. Cf., CIC, c., 1279. If funds are not available for the investigation, the Metropolitan shall make an immediate request for funding to the competent Roman congregation.

12   Cf. CIC, c. 142 §1; cf. CIC, c. 142 §1.

13   Cf. *As a Loving Mother*, 2-5.

of resolution by an administrative or penal process or other disposition, or the Holy See may return the case to the Metropolitan with further directions as to how to proceed.[14]

l)   Of course, unless otherwise established by special law, it pertains to the Roman Pontiff to make a final decision.[15]

Concluding remarks

What I present here is a framework for constructing new legal structures of accountability in the Church. This effort will require steadfast trust and openness in identifying, with the aid of everyone in the Church and with due regard for the diverse cultures and the universality of our Church, the legal and institutional pathways to safeguard young people in a just, compassionate, and robust manner.

Saint John Paul II spoke to this reality in his groundbreaking apostolic letter *Novo Millennio Ineunte*, when he observed that we need the wisdom of the law to provide precise rules to guarantee the participation of all the baptized, that rejects any arbitrariness, and is in keeping with our tradition of ordering Church life. At the same time, he emphasized, there is a correlative spirituality of communion that "supplies institutional reality with a soul" (n. 45).

We must move to establish robust laws and structures regarding the accountability of bishops precisely to supply with a new soul the institutional reality of the Church's discipline on sexual abuse.

In closing, I want to bring you back to that Memorial Mass that I celebrated in Chicago for the children and religious who had died in the fire at Our Lady of the Angels school. During the recessional hymn, the elderly immigrant mother who had spoken to me earlier, still holding firmly the *santino* in her hand, stopped me to tell me how comforted she was by the celebration, consoled that the Church had not forgotten her child. Then she did something quite extraordinary. She placed the *santino* in my

---

14   Cf. CIC, c. 1718; cf. *As a Loving Mother*, 2-5.

15   Cf., CIC, c. 1405; *As a Loving Mother*, 5.

hands, entrusting her child to the Church whom she recognized as Pietà, a loving mother. Sisters and brothers, we must work tirelessly in these days to justify that trust and honor such great faith.

Thank you for listening.

COMMUNION:
ACTING TOGETHER

LINDA GHISONI, *Undersecretary for the Laity of the Dicastery for the Laity, Family, and Life*

Introduction

"It is a new betrayal that comes from within the Church. These people are, to my eyes, howling wolves that penetrate the fold to further scare and disperse the flock, while they, the shepherds of the Church, should really be the ones who take care of the little ones and protect them."

In this witness of a female victim of abuse of conscience, power, and sexuality by priests, the "howling wolves" are the shepherds who denied *a priori* and who, even after the criminal facts were proven, made her an object of intimidation and annihilated her dignity, defining her as a person who, "at most, can pass between the painting and the wall" (useless and denied of all possibilities).

Listening to witnesses like her is not an exercise of commiseration, but an encounter with the flesh of Christ whose wounds are not healed, wounds which, as you said, Holy Father, cannot be fixed with a prescription.

How can we talk about the protection of minors in the Church without having present the victims and their families, the abusers, the accomplices, the deniers, those who are unjustly accused, the negligent, those who were ignored, who tried to speak and act but were silenced?

On our knees. This would be the appropriate posture for dealing with the topics of these days. Kneeling before the merciful Father, who sees the lacerated body of Christ, his Church, and sends us to take responsibility, as his People, for the wounds and to heal them with the balm of his love.

I have nothing to teach you, Your Holiness, Your Eminences, Your

Excellencies, Reverend Mothers and Reverend Fathers convened here. I believe rather that together, actively listening to each other, we commit ourselves to work so that in the future we no longer need such an extraordinary event as this meeting, and the Church, the People of God, will be cared for in a competent, responsible, and loving way, because of the people involved, because of what happened, so that prevention does not end up being just a beautiful program, but becomes an attitude in ordinary pastoral work.

Properly establishing accountability

In the face of inherent abnormality in every kind of abuse perpetrated against minors, we have, above all, a duty to know what happened, together with an awareness of its meaning, a duty of truth, of justice, of reparation and prevention, so that such abominations never happen again.

Knowledge of the abuses and of their nature is, obviously, the fundamental starting point, since it is not possible to prepare any prevention plan if we do not know what to avoid. However, knowledge of the facts and defining the nature of the phenomenon, although necessary and fundamental, "in itself is not enough."[1] To fulfill the above-mentioned demands of truth, justice, reparation, and prevention, what is required is the assumption of due responsibility on the part of those who are invested with it and the consequent duty to account for it; that is, what is required is *accountability*.

Accountability imposes a process of evaluation and reporting with respect to choices made and objectives identified and more or less realized. It responds to needs that are social in character, placing the person in responsibility in a position of reckoning not only to himself but also before the society in which he lives and for the benefit of which he is called to perform a specific role.

However, accountability in the Church, contrary to what it may seem, does not respond primarily to social and organizational needs. And not

---

1   Pope Francis, Letter to the People of God (August 20, 2018), n. 2.

even—always in the first place—to the need for transparency, to which we are all called to pay special attention for reasons of truth.

Such needs, not to be neglected or minimized, are just, because the Church cannot be separated from what its institutional dimension requires, but these social aspects are not the foundation of accountability, which is found instead in the nature of the Church as mystery of communion.

We know that the nature of the Church as communion emerges especially thanks to the Second Vatican Council, although, in truth, neither the Dogmatic Constitution *Lumen Gentium* nor the other ecclesiological documents seem to explicitly express the ecclesiology of communion.

It was necessary to await the extraordinary Synod of Bishops of the year 1985—convened to "meditate upon, deepen, and promote the application of the teachings of Vatican II twenty years after its conclusion"[2]— to elaborate the category of communion as an interpretative key of the Church in the light of revelation. This emerges from the first, direct, foundational reference to the sacramental dimension of the Church, to that Trinitarian mystery in which the Church recognizes its own face, though in a sacramental and therefore analogical form: "*veluti sacramentum*," "as a sign and instrument of a very closely knit union with God and of the unity of the whole human race" (LG 1).

Based solely on such a foundation, all action in the Church acquires its full meaning: even an action that bears a distinctly social character, such as accountability, must be understood in its relation to the nature of the Church itself, and to its dimension of communion.

What can this mean in our specific context?

Not infrequently, I sense an impatience in the Church over the attention that is dedicated to the issue of sexual abuse of minors. A priest, a few days ago, exclaimed, "Still? We continue talking about abuse! The Church's attention to this topic is exaggerated."

Even a practicing lady told me candidly, "It is better not to talk about these matters, because it fosters a distrust of the Church. Talking about it

---

2   Pope John Paul II, Address at the Conclusion of the Second Extraordinary Assembly of the Synod of Bishops (December 7, 1985).

obscures all the good done in the parishes. Let it be handled by the pope, the bishops, and the priests among themselves."

Talking about it—and not just about the abuses themselves, but also about conscience, power, sexuality—obscures the good that is lived in the parishes?!

To these people—and first of all to myself—I say that becoming aware of the phenomenon and understanding one's responsibility is not a fixation. It is not an accessory inquisitorial activity to satisfy mere social needs, but an exigency stemming from the very nature of the Church as a mystery of communion founded in the Trinity, as the People of God on its journey, that does not avoid, but confronts, with renewed communal awareness, even the challenges related to the abuses occurring within it, to the detriment of its youngest, undermining and breaking this communion.

Some consequent ecclesiological questions

Only by starting from a vision of the Church as a sacrament that manifests the mystery of the Trinitarian communion is it possible to understand correctly the variety of charisms, gifts, and ministries in the Church, the variety of roles and functions of the People of God.

1. The first crucial question that derives from what has been said is the following. The faithful in the Church are not assigned roles and tasks on a social distributive basis in the interest of institutional functioning. We know well that the common priesthood of the faithful, founded on baptism, makes Christians participants, precisely by virtue of baptism, in the triple *munus* of Christ the priest, king, and prophet (see LG 10). The honest reference, therefore, to the Church as communion, as People of God on journey, demands and urges that all the members of this People, each in their own way, live consequently the rights and duties to which they have been made to partake in baptism. It is not a matter of grabbing places or jobs or of sharing power: the call to be People of God gives us a mission that everyone is called to live according to the gifts received, not alone, but precisely as a People.

2. A second important question in the context of our discourse concerns the correct understanding of the ordained ministry, especially in the relationship between the bishop and priests. If on the one hand priests are required to be united to their bishop with sincere love and obedience, recognizing in him the authority of Christ as supreme Pastor, nonetheless the bishops, as written in Decree *Presbyterorum Ordinis*, should "be concerned as far as they are able for [their priests'] material and especially for their spiritual well-being. For above all upon the bishops rests the heavy responsibility for the sanctity of their priests. Therefore, they should exercise the greatest care in the continual formation of their priests" (n. 7). A correct relationship between the bishop and priests leads to a real material and spiritual attentiveness to the priests by the bishop, on whom lies in the first place the responsibility for their sanctity.

It is necessary that the priestly ministry, at every level, avail itself of a solid formation, that it may be lived for what it is, that is, as dedication and service to Christ and the Church, washing feet as Jesus did to the apostles, disappointing many of his contemporaries because he did not exercise the power they expected. The priestly ministry, when it is lived as such, preserves one from every temptation of the caress of power, of self-referentiality and self-complacency, of principality and exploitation of others to cultivate one's own pleasure at all levels, even sexual.

So many priests, so many bishops, edify us with their ministry, with their life of prayer, dedication, and service, establishing healthy, free relations within the People of God. To these priests we offer our thanks, encouraging them and supporting them in their life of holiness and service in the vineyard of the Lord to which they are called!

3. A further point to be noted, which derives from the vision of the Church as communion, the People of God on their journey, is need for interaction between the various charisms and ministries. The Church becomes visible and active in her nature as communion if each baptized person lives and does what is proper to him, if the diversity of charisms and ministries is expressed in the necessary cooperation of each one, while respecting differences. The aforementioned conciliar document of 1965 dedicated to

priests stipulated not only that "priests must sincerely acknowledge and promote the dignity of the laity and the part proper to them in the mission of the Church." It also urged them to "willingly listen to the laity, consider their wants in a fraternal spirit, recognize their experience and competence in the different areas of human activity, so that together with them they will be able to recognize the signs of the times." In addition, it said, "they should confidently entrust to the laity duties in the service of the Church, allowing them freedom and room for action; in fact, they should invite them on suitable occasions to undertake worlds on their own initiative" (PO 9).

Starting from the *communio* that constitutes the Church, a necessary diversified contribution of all becomes clear, not so that someone can claim their leading role, but to make visible the multifaceted richness of the Church in respect of the *proprium* of everyone, against the claim that the charism of synthesis is the synthesis of the charisms.

4. Finally, we must note that the involvement of the whole People of God is necessarily dynamic. The laity and the consecrated are not to be mere executors of orders by clerics, but all are servants in the one vineyard, in which each person offers his own contribution to become involved in the discernment that the Spirit suggests to the Church. Undoubtedly, the ordained ministry, in its highest degree, the episcopal one, bears upon itself the responsibility of making the ultimate decision, by virtue of the power it is recognized to have, but it cannot act alone or limit to a few its work of discernment. It will be vital for the bishops to avail themselves of the contributions, the counsel, and the discernment of everyone in the Church, including the laity, is capable of, not only for themselves and for their personal choices, but as a Church and for the good of the Church in the *hic et nunc* in which they are called to live.

It is always the nature of the Church as communion that shows us the way and the method, in this case a dynamism of involvement of the whole People of God that leads to living, walking together, synodality as a shared process, in which each one has a different part, diversified responsibilities, but all constitute the one Church. As we read in the apostolic constitution *Episcopalis Communio* of September 15, 2018, "Indeed, 'the universal body made up of the faithful, whom the Holy One has anointed (cf. 1 John 2:20, 27), is incapable of erring in belief. This is a property that belongs to the people as a whole; a supernatural sense of faith is the means by which they make this property manifest, when "from Bishops to the last of the lay faithful, 'they show universal agreement in matters of faith and morals' (LG 12)....A Bishop who lives among his faithful has his ears open to listen to 'what the Spirit says to the churches' (Rev 2:7), and to the 'voice of the sheep,' also through those diocesan institutions whose task it is to advise the Bishop, promoting a loyal and constructive dialogue."

These reflections invite us to avoid two erroneous positions.

A bishop cannot think that matters concerning the Church can be resolved by him acting alone or exclusively among peers, according to the refrain, "Only a bishop can know what is good for bishops," or, similarly, "Only a priest knows what is good for priests," "only a layperson for lay-people," "only a woman for women," and so on.

Likewise, we can say that it is erroneous, in my view, to argue that the involvement of the laity as such in matters that touch the ordained ministers is a guarantee of greater correctness, as they would be "third parties" with respect to events. Some have suggested, "Let us set up a commission of laymen because it is more credible than a commission of priests, who tend to be less objective, to cover-up and defend a priori."

As a lay woman, a wife, and a mother, I must honestly note that among the laity, just as among the priests and religious, there can be and there are people who are not free, but would be willing to participate in cover-ups with someone instead of serving the Church lovingly, intelligently, and freely and being faithful to their own vocation.

Returning to the nature of the Church as communion—where we can see the diversity of charisms and ministries does not mean a weakening but brings wealth and strength—helps to find the reasons to avoid these extreme and unproductive slogans.

Ideas for some practical implementation

Having briefly presented these fundamentals and issues, this meeting gives us the opportunity to know what is being done in the Church, what is to be implemented, aware that if it is true that this meeting convened by the pope does not constitute the point of arrival of a completed and perfect journey, It is equally true that it is not a starting point, as if we can ignore the normative, pastoral interventions of the magisterium that have already been offered and the numerous actions that have been taken.

1. The first idea is therefore the knowledge and study of what is already tested and effective, promoted in other ecclesial contexts, by other episcopates. I refer to practices that call for the involvement of competent people who represent the whole People of God because every baptized person, animated by the Spirit, is able to express a *sensus fidei* that the Church cannot ignore. In this context it is good to recognize the work of those who, in recent years, have dedicated their intelligence, hearts, and hands to this cause by listening to the victims, developing protocols, guidelines, reviews, and so on, drawing on specific skills from the whole People of God.

Given the diversity of various cultural and social contexts in which the Church is present, there should not be a "business class" of some particular churches and an "economy class" of others, but the one Church of Christ expressed everywhere, guaranteeing to everyone everywhere the tools, procedures, criteria that—beyond the necessary local peculiarities—protect minors, pursue truth and justice, promote reparation, and prevent sexual abuse.

2. In the national guidelines, a specific chapter should be inserted that determines reasons and procedures of accountability. The bishops and religious superiors should establish a standard procedure for verifying the accomplishment of what is called for and reasons for the actions taken or not, so that there is not a need later to justify a given behavior, subjecting it to the needs of the moment, perhaps related to a defensive action. To establish a standard procedure of verification should not be misun-

derstood as a lack of trust toward the superior or the bishop. Rather it ought to be understood as an aid that allows him to focus, first of all for himself and at the right moment (that is, when all the elements are clear and concurrent), the reason for a certain action taken or omitted. To say that the bishop must always give a report of his work to someone does not mean subjecting him to a control or putting him in a position of *a priori* distrust, but engaging him in the dynamics of ecclesial communion where all the members act in a coordinated way, according to their own charisms and ministries. If a priest offers an account to the community, to his fellow priests, and to his bishop for his work, to whom does a bishop offer account? To what accountability is he subject? Identifying an objective method of accountability not only does not weaken his authority; it gives value to him as shepherd of a flock, in his own function that is not separated from the people for whom he is called to give life. It may also happen, as for each of us, that "giving report" leads to awareness of an error, making clear a wrong path taken, even if in a given moment one thought, mistakenly, to be acting for the good. This will not constitute a judgment from which to defend oneself in order to recover credit, a stain on one's own honorability, a threat to one's own ordinary and immediate power (cf. *Christus Dominus*, n. 8a). On the contrary, this will be the witness of a journey made together, which alone can provide the discernment of truth, justice, and charity. The logic of communion is not an accusation and a defense, but a working together ("*con-correre*" precisely, only in communion) for the good of all. Accountability is therefore a form, even more necessary today, in this logic of communion. To start locally, on a diocesan or regional level, with advisors that operate in a co-responsible manner with the bishops and religious superiors, supporting them in this task with competence and acting as a means of verification and discernment of the initiatives to be undertaken, while never substituting for the bishop or superior or engaging in decisions that fall under their direct jurisdictional responsibility, can be an example and a model of a healthy collaboration of laity, religious, and clergy in the life of the Church.

3. It is desirable that in the territory of each episcopal conference, independent consultative commissions are to be created to advise and assist the bishops and religious superiors and to promote a uniform level of responsibility in the various dioceses. These commissions should be composed of lay people, without excluding religious and clerics. It would not be a case of people who judge the bishops, but of faithful who give their advice and assistance to the pastors, evaluating their work with gospel criteria, and who also inform the faithful of the territory about the appropriate procedures. These national advisory committees, in turn, through regular reports and meetings, can contribute to ensuring greater uniformity of practices and an increasingly effective approach, so that particular churches learn from each other in the spirit of mutual trust and communion, with the aim of actively taking on and sharing concern for the smallest and most vulnerable.

4. It is opportune to consider the creation of a central office—not of accountability, which is to be evaluated on a local level—to promote the formation of these organisms with a properly ecclesial identity, promoting and verifying regularly the correct functioning of what happens at the local level, with attention to correctness from the ecclesiological point of view, in a way that the charisms and ministries in the group are all adequately represented and each one can contribute with their own specific participation while preserving the liberty of each other.

5. Current legislation on the pontifical secret ought to be revised, in a way that it protects the values it intends to protect—namely, the dignity of the persons involved, the good reputation of each, and the good of the Church—but at the same time allows for the development of a climate of greater transparency and trust, avoiding the idea that the secret is intended to hide problems rather than to protect legitimate values.

6. It will also be necessary to refine criteria for a correct communication in a time like ours in which the requirements of transparency must be balanced with those of confidentiality. Indeed, both unjustified confiden-

tiality and uncontrolled disclosure both risk generating bad communication and failing to render a service to the truth. Accountability also means knowing how to communicate. If one does not communicate, how can one be accountable to others? And then what communion can there be among us?

Conclusion

These considerations just mentioned regarding the possible actions to be performed as Church, as People of God in communion and with co-responsibility, are nothing more than suggestions for reflection and comparison, especially in group discussion, in order to stimulate insights and concrete applications. In fact, as the "Letter to the People of God" urges us, "Today we are challenged as the People of God to take on the pain of our brothers and sisters wounded in their flesh and in their spirit. If, in the past, the response was one of omission, today we want solidarity, in the deepest and most challenging sense, to become our way of forging present and future history" (n. 2).

INTERVENTION OF
HIS HOLINESS POPE FRANCIS

Listening to Dr. Ghisoni, I heard the Church speak about herself. That is, we have all spoken about the Church. In all of the interventions. But this time it was the Church herself who spoke. It is not just a question of style: the feminine genius, reflected in the Church, which is woman.

Inviting a woman to speak is not to enter into the mode of an ecclesiastical feminism, because in the end every feminism ends up being machismo with a skirt. No. Inviting a woman to speak about the wounds of the Church is to invite the Church to speak about herself, about the wounds she has. And this I believe is the step that we must take with great determination: woman is the image of the Church that is woman, bride, mother. A style. Without this style we will speak of the People of God, but as an organization, perhaps a trade union, but not as a family born of the Mother Church.

The logic of Dr. Ghisoni's thought was precisely that of a mother, and it ended with the story of what happens when a woman gives birth to a child. It is the feminine mystery of the Church that is bride and mother. It is not of giving more functions to women in the Church—yes, this is good, but that is not how the problem is solved—it is a question of integrating the woman as the image of the Church into our thinking...and also of thinking of the Church with the categories of a woman. Thank you for your testimony.

TESTIMONIAL

OF A VICTIM

OF SEXUAL ABUSE

WE MUST BEGIN AGAIN TOGETHER

Good evening. I wanted to tell you about when I was a child. But there's no point, because when I was eleven years old, a priest from my parish destroyed my life. Since then I, who loved coloring books and doing somersaults on the grass, have not existed.

Instead, engraved in my eyes, ears, nose, body, and soul, are all the times he immobilized me, the child, with superhuman strength: I desensitized myself, I held my breath, I came out of my body, I searched desperately for a window to look out of, waiting for it all to end. I thought, "If I don't move, maybe I won't feel anything; if I don't breathe, maybe I could die."

When it did end, I would take back what was my wounded and humiliated body, and I would leave, even believing I had imagined it all. But how could I, a child, understand what had happened? I thought, "It must have been my fault!" or "Maybe I deserved this bad thing?"

These thoughts are the worst wounds that the abuse, and the abuser, insinuates into your heart, more than the wounds that lacerate your body. I felt I wasn't worth anything anymore. I felt I didn't even exist. I just wanted to die. I tried to…but I couldn't.

The abuse went on for five years. No one noticed.

While I did not speak, my body did: eating disorders, various periods in hospital: everything screamed that I was sick. While I, completely alone, kept my pain to myself. They thought I was anxious about school where, suddenly, I was performing really badly.

Then, the first time I fell in love…My heart beating with emotion and struggling against the same heart that palpitated remembering the horror it had experienced; gestures of tenderness against acts of force: impossible comparisons. Awareness becomes an unbearable reality! So as not to feel the pain, the disgust, the confusion, the fear, the shame, the powerlessness, the impotence, my mind removed the facts as they happened, it numbed my body by putting emotional distance between everything I was living. And this provoked enormous damage.

When I was twenty-six, I gave birth for the first time. Flashbacks and images brought everything back to me. My labor was interrupted, my child was in danger; breastfeeding was impossible because of the terrible memories that emerged. I thought I had gone mad. So I confided in my husband, a confidence that was used against me during our separation, when, citing the abuse I had suffered, he asked that I be denied parental authority because I was an unworthy mother. What followed was the patient listening of a dear friend, and the courage to write a letter to that priest, which concluded with the promise never again to concede to him the power of my silence.

From then, until today, I continue to go through a very difficult process of re-elaboration that has no shortcuts, that requires enormous perseverance in rebuilding my identity, dignity, and faith. It is a journey undertaken mostly alone, and with the help of a specialist, if possible. Abuse causes immediate damage, but not only that: what is most difficult is dealing daily with that experience that attacks you and presents itself in the most unexpected moments. You have to live with it…forever! All you can do, if you can, is learn how to hurt yourself less.

Inside you, there are endless questions you will never be able to answer, because abuse makes no sense!

"Why me?" I used to ask, and not because I would have preferred it to happen to someone else, because what I suffered would be too much for anyone else! Or: "Where were you, God?" How I cried over this question! I no longer trusted Man and God, in the good Father who protects the small and the weak. As a little girl, I was certain nothing bad could come from a man who had the "odor" of God! How could the same hands, that had dared touch me like that, offer blessing and the Eucharist? He was an adult and I was a child. He had taken advantage of his power as well as his position: a true abuse of faith!

And last but not least: How was I to overcome my anger and not leave the Church after such an experience, especially in the face of such terrible incoherence between what my abuser preached and what he did? And what about those who, before these crimes, belittled, hid, silenced, or worse still, failed to defend the little ones, evil-mindedly limiting themselves to moving priests so they could cause harm somewhere else? In the face of this, we innocent victims feel the pain that killed us, even more intensely: this too is an abuse of our human dignity, of our conscience, as well as of our faith!

We victims, if we can find the strength to speak out or expose, must find the courage to do so, knowing that we risk not being believed or seeing our abuser getting away with a small canonical penalty. This cannot and must not be the case anymore!

It took me forty years to find the strength to speak out. I wanted to break the silence that nourishes every form of abuse; I wanted to start again from an act of truth, acknowledging that this act also offers an opportunity to the person who abused me. I experienced the process of speaking out at a very high emotional cost: talking to six very sensitive people, but all of them men and all of them priests, was hard. I think that the presence of a woman is a necessary and indispensable gesture in order to welcome, listen, and accompany us victims.

Being believed, and knowing him sentenced, gave me a reality check: that part of me that always hoped the abuse never really happened had to admit defeat, but at the same time, it received a caress: now I know I am something else. I am not just the abuse I suffered and the scars I carry.

The Church can be proud of being able to proceed despite the statute of limitations (a right that is denied by the Italian justice system), but not of the fact of recognizing as a mitigating factor, for the abuser, the length of time between the offense and the accusation (as in my case). Victims are not guilty of their silence! The trauma and damage they suffer are all the greater the longer the period of silence: the victim spends that time between fear, shame, denial, and a sense of helplessness. Wounds can never be prescribed. On the contrary!

Today I am here, and together with me are all the abused boys and girls, all the women and men, trying to be reborn from their wounds. But, above all, there are also those who tried and did not make it. It is from here, with them in our hearts, that we must start again, together.

Transparency

PRESENTATIONS

OPENNESS TO THE WORLD

As a Consequence of the Ecclesial Mission

Sr. Veronica Openibo, SHCJ,
Society of the Holy Child Jesus

Papa Francesco,
My brothers and sisters, good morning.

I begin this talk with a quotation from Luke, chapter 4. For me "Openness to the World as a Consequence of the Ecclesial Mission" is the mission statement of Jesus, that we also follow. "The Spirit of the Lord is upon me and anointed me to preach good news to the poor. The Spirit has sent me to proclaim deliverance to the captives and recovery of sight to the blind, to release the oppressed, to proclaim the Lord's year of favor" (Luke 4:18–19).

Abstract

As a result of the self-understanding of her mission in the world today, the Church needs to update and create new systems and practices that will promote action without fear of making mistakes. Clerical sex abuse is a crisis that has reduced the credibility of the Church when transparency should be the hallmark of mission as followers of Jesus Christ. The fact that many accuse the Catholic Church today of negligence is disturbing. The Church must do everything possible to protect its young and vulnerable members. The focus should not to be on fear or disgrace but rather on the Church's mission to serve with integrity and justice.

Introduction

The mission of the Church flows directly from our deepest understanding of the Incarnation. Catholic Christianity is grounded in belief in a God who chose to be one with the human world.

The self-understanding of the mission of the Church must be a manifestation of the Christ we know as both human and divine. The whole of Christ's mission was to reveal who God is and who we can become. This implies a total acceptance of all that is human and all that the power of God's grace does to transform us into being witnesses of the divine. Our world view, if Christian, must be based on respect and dignity for each human being.

At the present time, we are in a state of crisis and shame. We have seriously clouded the grace of the Christ-mission. Is it possible for us to move from fear of scandal to truth? How do we remove the masks that hide our sinful neglect? What policies, programs, and procedures will bring us to a new, revitalized starting point characterized by a transparency that lights up the world with God's hope for us in building the Reign of God?

Throughout the time of writing this presentation, my eyes were cloudy and I wondered what this could mean. Then I remembered the first time I watched the movie *Spotlight*, the 2015 American biographical drama about the investigation by the *Boston Globe* into cases of widespread and systemic child sex abuse in the Boston area by numerous priests and the alleged cover-up by ecclesial authorities.

At the end of the film was a long list of cases and the dioceses where they occurred and reading about the number of children affected (and later seeing the vast amount of money spent on settlements), tears of sorrow flowed. How could the clerical Church have kept silent, covering these atrocities? The silence, the carrying of the secrets in the hearts of the perpetrators, the length of the abuses and the constant transfers of perpetrators are unimaginable. Presumably there were significant signs in the confessional and in spiritual direction. With a heavy and sad heart, I think of all the atrocities we have committed as members of the Church. The Constitutions of my own congregation reminds me: "In Christ we unite ourselves to the whole of humanity, especially to the poor and suffering.

We accept our share of responsibility for the sin of the world and so live that his love may prevail" (SHCJ Constitutions, n. 6). We must acknowledge that our mediocrity, hypocrisy, and complacency have brought us to this disgraceful and scandalous place we find ourselves as a Church. We pause to pray: Lord, have mercy on us!

In *Gaudete et Exsultate* (n. 164), we read that "those who think they commit no grievous sins against God's law can fall into a state of dull lethargy. Since they see nothing serious to reproach themselves with, they fail to realize that their spiritual life has gradually turned lukewarm. They end up weakened and corrupted." So many aspects of this statement from Pope Francis stand out for me on the issue of child abuse, as also these sentences from the PCB Preparation Document: "A Church that is closed/shut off is no longer Church. Her mission would be thwarted. It's not about giving up principles and secularizing the Church, it's about living visibly and perceptibly what you claim to be, or what and how you really are."

We proclaim the Ten Commandments and "parade ourselves" as being the custodians of moral standards/values and good behavior in society. Hypocrites at times? Yes! Why did we keep silent for so long? How can we turn this around for a time to evangelize, catechize, and educate all the members of the Church, including clergy and religious? Is it true that most bishops did nothing about the sexual abuse of children? Some did and some did not out of fear or cover-up.

We might say the Church is now taking steps to arrest the situation but also to be more transparent about all the steps it had been taking privately over two decades, such as meeting with victims of sexual abuse, reporting cases to the appropriate civil authorities, and setting up commissions. The question today is more about how to address the issue of the sexual abuse of minors more directly, transparently, and courageously as a Church. The hierarchical structure and systems in the Church should be a blessing for us to reach the whole world with very clear mechanisms to address this and many other issues. Why has this not happened enough? Why have other issues around sexuality not been addressed sufficiently, e.g., misuse of power, money, clericalism, gender discrimination, the role of women and the laity in general? Is it that the hierarchical structures and long protocols that negatively affected swift actions focused more on media reactions?

Reflection

I would like to offer some reflections based on my experience as an African woman religious. I have lived in Rome for fifteen years and studied in America for three. So, I am familiar with these issues in the Global North. Probably like many of you, I have heard some Africans and Asians say that "this is not our issue in countries in Africa and Asia; it is the problem in Europe, the Americas, Canada and Australia." However, I worked throughout Nigeria in the area of sexuality education for nine years and heard the stories and counseled many people. I realized how serious the issues were and still are, and sharing a few of my personal experiences emphasizes this fact. In the early 1990s, a priest told me there were sexual abuses in the convents and formation houses and that, as president of the Nigeria Conference of Women Religious, I should, please, do something to address the issue. A second priest in the early 2000s said that a particular ethnic group practiced a lot of incest, but I added that from my personal experience incest is a world issue. A dying old man revealed to me he was acting strangely because of the sexual abuse he experienced as a teenager from the priests in his school. A thirteen-year-old girl met her priest attacker twenty-five years later and he did not recognize her...

Transparency

Let us not hide such events anymore because of the fear of making mistakes. Too often we want to keep silent until the storm has passed! This storm will not pass by. Our credibility is at stake. Jesus told us, "Whoever causes one of these little ones who believe [in me] to sin, it would be better for him if a great millstone were put around his neck and he were thrown into the sea" (Mark 9:42). We must face this issue and seek healing for the victims of abuse. The normal process for clergy—in the past and still in the present in some areas—was/is to give support to "one of us," to avoid exposing a scandal and bringing discredit to the Church. All offenders, regardless of their clerical status, found guilty, should be given the same penalty for the abuse of minors.

Let us have courageous conversations rather than saying nothing to avoid making a mistake. We can make a mistake, but we are not created to be a mistake and posterity will judge us for not taking action. The first step toward true transparency is to admit wrongdoing and then to publish what has been done since the time of Pope John Paul II to heal the situation. It may not be sufficient in the eyes of many, but it will show that the Church had not been totally silent.

We must build more effective and efficient processes, based on research in human development as well as civil and canon law, for the safeguarding of minors. Then clear and comprehensive safeguarding policies and guidelines in every diocese should be placed visibly in various parish offices and published on the internet. There must be better handling of the cases through face-to-face, transparent, and courageous conversations with both victims and offenders, as well as investigating groups. In some parts of the world, including countries in Africa and Asia, not saying anything is a terrible mistake, as we have seen in many countries. The fact that there are huge issues of poverty, illness, war, and violence in some countries in the Global South does not mean that the area of sexual abuse should be downplayed or ignored. The Church has to be proactive in facing it.

The excuse that respect be given to some priests by virtue of their advanced years and hierarchical position is unacceptable. This argument states that many of the criminal offenders are old, some no longer alive, and that we should not hurt them or their reputations by taking away their priesthood in old age. We can feel sad for those who, when they were younger, committed offenses that are now being brought out to the open. But my heart bleeds for many of the victims who have lived with the misplaced shame and guilt of repeated violations for years. In some of these cases, the offenders did not even see these victims as persons but as objects.

It is true, as a Church, that we believe in repentance of the sinner, in conversion of hearts and the grace of transformation, "Go and from now on do not sin any more," says Jesus (John 8:1–11). This can create a strong dilemma for some, especially when we know that abusers have often been victims themselves. Do we need to probe deeply what we mean by justice with compassion? How can we help create the environment for prayer and discernment for the grace of God to enlighten us in the way of justice so that transformation and healing may take place for both victims and offenders? We would need to find out where throughout the world (not only in wealthier countries) are the best practices for doing this being developed, and can we implement them? Many of these are to be found within the Church.

In publishing the names of offenders, can we publish a complete set of information regarding these situations?

Strategic way forward

1. It is becoming evident that for many victims, being listened to and helped psychologically and spiritually was the beginning of a healing process. Can we train enough sensitive and compassionate people to offer this service in all countries, including those places struggling to put food on the table? Are there ways of helping parishes heal victims using their traditional wisdom? Do we make use of preaching and other means to address sexual issues in society? How might dioceses share in a strategic way in providing culturally sensitive education programs and training kits? Such materials, respecting the dignity of the human persons and emphasizing unacceptable behaviors, could be used in parishes and schools, hospitals, and other places of pastoral ministry.

2. How can we continue to address in very concrete ways the issues of prostitution and trafficking on an immense scale, as well as personal infidelity and promiscuity around the world? There must be Catholics, alongside others with similar principles, in positions of influence in, for example, the film industry, TV, and advertising. They could be

encouraged to come together and reflect on their role in promoting a better view of the human person. Let there be a focus on society's disservice to men in every patriarchal culture in the area of sexuality. Let us investigate how better to use social media to educate people on the whole area of sexuality and human relationships.

3. Essential, surely, is a clear and balanced education and training about sexuality and boundaries in the seminaries and formation houses; in the ongoing formation of priests, religious men and women, and bishops. It worries me when I see, in Rome and elsewhere, the youngest seminarians being treated as though they are more special than everyone else, thus encouraging them to assume, from the beginning of their training, exalted ideas about their status. The study of human development must give rise to a serious question about the existence of minor seminaries. The formation of young women religious, too, can often lead to a false sense of superiority over their lay sisters and brothers, that their calling is a "higher" one. What damage has that thinking done to the mission of the Church? Have we forgotten the reminder by Vatican II in *Gaudium et Spes* of the universal call to holiness? In addition, we need to ask responsible and sensitive lay people and women religious to give true and honest evaluation of candidates for episcopal appointments.

4. Could each diocese be challenged to gather men and women of integrity—laity, including religious, and clergy—to form a joint commission sharing expertise about the documentary procedures and protocols, the legal and financial implications of allegations, and the necessary channels of responsibility and accountability? A well-qualified person—lay, religious, or priest—is likely to be the best chairperson of such a group. In addition, they need to work out how best to face the serious issues of sexual abuse already exploding in some Asian and African countries in the same way that it has elsewhere. Many people who were sexually abused by priests or others in pastoral

positions will suffer as traumatic memories are evoked. Some people will be reminded that they could well be revealed as former or current abusers or accused of covering up such facts. Many in various forms of ministry will come across people, family members, adults and/or children, who have been or are being abused and need to know how to respond appropriately. Some allegations will be false, which causes suffering of another kind. The impact of damaged faith in the Church cannot be under-emphasized, as a large number of Catholics are and will be angry and confused. People in positions of some authority also need to know what to say or do in terms of response when issues get to the media.

Conclusion

We know that the greatest issue is the proclamation of the gospel in a way that will touch the hearts of the young and old. We are called to proclaim the good news, but we must BE good news to the people we serve today. No wonder Pope Francis has declared the month of October 2019 to be an Extraordinary Missionary Month.

The Church in its mission from Jesus Christ must be open to greater transparency because we are sent to the world locally and globally. Our whole being is not just about keeping the faith, but living visibly and distinctively what we claim to be. We are called like Jesus in his mission statement: "The Spirit of the Lord is upon me and anointed me to preach good news to the poor. The Spirit has sent me to proclaim deliverance to the captives and recovery of sight to the blind, to release the oppressed, to proclaim the Lord's year of favor" (Luke 4:18–19).

As an indicator or postscript, I emphasize the following: *The Spirit of the Lord is upon* each of us here, *has anointed* all of us, *to preach good news to the poor*, the vulnerable, protecting especially defenseless children, seeking justice for the victims of abuse, and taking steps to prevent this abuse from recurring, *to proclaim deliverance to the captives* the perpetrators are in need of deliverance, conversion, and transformation, *and recovery of sight* to the blind, those who are not seeing the issues, or focusing on protecting "our own," or keeping silent or covering up, need recovery of sight, *to release the oppressed and to proclaim the Lord's year of favor* by taking the necessary steps and maintaining zero tolerance with regard to sexual abuse we will release the oppressed. This is our year of favor; let us courageously take up the responsibility to be truly transparent and accountable.

Returning to the title of this conference, another self-understanding passages is from Matthew 5:14–16: "You are the light of the world. A city set on a mountain cannot be hidden. Nor do they light a lamp and then put it under a bushel basket; it is set on a lampstand, where it gives light to all in the house. Just so, your light must shine before others, that they may see your good deeds and glorify your heavenly Father."

I read with great interest many articles about the pope's reactions in the case of the Chilean bishops—from a denial of accusations, to anger because of deception and cover-up, to the acceptance of resignations of three of the bishops. I admire you, Brother Francis, for taking time as a true Jesuit to discern and be humble enough to change your mind, to apologize, and to take action—an example for all of us.

Thank you, Pope Francis, for providing this opportunity for us to check and see where we have acted strangely, ignorantly, secretly, and complacently. I believe we will change, with great determination, our total approach to reporting abuse, to supporting the victims, to getting the right people to mentor and give support to victims, and, above all, to doing what we can to protect minors and vulnerable adults from any form of abuse. Thank you, too, for providing women religious, through the executive of the Union of Superiors General (UISG), an opportunity to participate in this conference. Women have acquired a lot of useful experience to offer in this field and have already done much to support victims and also to work creatively on their own use of power and authority.

I hope and pray that at the end of this conference we will choose deliberately to break any culture of silence and secrecy among us, to allow more light into our Church. Let us acknowledge our vulnerability, be proactive, not reactive, in combating the challenges facing the world of the young and the vulnerable, and look fearlessly into other issues of abuse in the Church and society.

May I remind all of us of Pope Francis' own words: A Christian who does not move forward has an identity that is "not well...The Gospel is clear: the Lord sent them out saying: go, go forward!...The Christian walks, moves past difficulties and announces that the kingdom of God is near."[1]

Thank you.

---

1   Morning Meditation in the Chapel of the *Domus Sanctae Marthae* (February 14, 2014).

TRANSPARENCY AS A COMMUNITY OF BELIEVERS

CARDINAL REINHARD MARX, *Archbishop of Munich and Freising, President of the German Bishops' Conference*

Holy Father,

Your Eminences, your Excellencies, dear sisters and brothers,

When I speak to you today about transparency, then I do this under two conditions. First, on condition of a specific understanding of the concept of transparency. I understand this not as the greatest possible mass of diverse, uncoordinated information disclosed. For me, transparency means that actions, decisions, processes, procedures, etc. are understandable and traceable. I believe that traceability and transparency are inextricably linked.

Second, I speak to you about transparency in relation to traceability as a cardinal who is German. Perhaps some of you will now immediately think: typical, actually one cannot expect anything else. We Germans are known for a certain tendency toward administration, which includes these already-mentioned aspects of traceability and transparency. Files, documents, forms, guidelines, paragraphs, lists, procedural rules, and the like—these seem to be handed down to Germans from birth, and anyone who somehow has to do with us also seems in some way to be confronted with all these things I have just mentioned. Some people may consider this as a certain quirkiness and not pay further attention to it. Others—perhaps even the majority—may be opposed to all of this. They ask themselves seriously: Is this administration not contrary to the dynamics of life? Is it not clear to them, that administration puts files in focus, instead of people and their needs? Is it not true that administration only creates additional work and distracts from the real tasks?

I would like to address these questions with you. And don't worry—this is not a problem just for Germans, Swiss, or Americans. It is a fundamental problem, which we all have to face together as a Church, especially and specifically regarding appropriate handling of the topic of abuse. It is important to clarify how much administration the Church needs. And at first glance, it seems rather that less is required.

This assumption can be based on numerous aspects. Faith cannot be administered. The Spirit of God cannot possibly be captured in a file or folder. God's love is reflected in specific acts of caring for the people, rather than in administrative documents. Prayer is much stronger than any number of administrative procedures. The sacraments convey true mercy, while administration remains part of the minutiae of this world. One could enumerate further arguments to show that administration doesn't actually fit so well in the Church, and can more or less be neglected. But is that really true? Let us attempt to clarify this, by going through the following thought processes together, and becoming conscious of: what constitutes the Church; what role should administration play; how does administration fulfill its purpose; what must be attended to, so that the required prerequisites are in place; and what are the resulting tasks?

Even here, however, I cannot conceal what I am firmly convinced of and what I think is essential: administration within the area of responsibility of the Church is not only a technical, specialist, or functional issue. Such administration within the Church is closely related to theological fundamentals, is theologically-spiritually motivated, and is closely linked with the specific actions of the Church. A fully functional Church administration is an important building block in the fight against abuse and in dealing with abuse. Why this is so, in my opinion, will be shown in the following sections.

The Church's understanding of itself

The Church has a mission in this world. As the Dogmatic Constitution on the Church *Lumen Gentium* says right at the beginning, "The Church is in Christ like a sacrament or as a sign and instrument both of a very closely knit union with God and of the unity of the whole human race" (LG 1). This mission is fulfilled by specific people in specific locations under very specific conditions, which also requires appropriate, tangible, worldly means. Therefore, it is for good reason that a little further in the text of *Lumen Gentium* it states, "Christ, the one Mediator, established and continually sustains here on earth His holy Church, the community of faith, hope and charity, as an entity with visible delineation…But, the society structured with hierarchical organs and the Mystical Body of Christ, are not to be considered as two realities, nor are the visible assembly and the spiritual community, nor the earthly Church and the Church enriched with heavenly things; rather they form one complex reality which coalesces from a divine and a human element" (LG 8). And it then goes on to say, "For this reason, by no weak analogy, it [the Church] is compared to the mystery of the incarnate Word. As the assumed nature inseparably united to Him, serves the divine Word as a living organ of salvation, so, in a similar way, does the visible social structure of the Church serve the Spirit of Christ, who vivifies it, in the building up of the body."

Briefly summarized, this means: the actions of the Church in this world cannot be strictly and solely spiritual. Neglecting the worldly aspects of the Church and its own laws does not do justice to the reality of the Church. In an analogous way, the body of Christ and the human organization of the Church must be seen "without separation and without intermingling." Therefore, all the basic principles for a good society and a people-serving organization in the life of the Church cannot be ignored.

The purpose of administration

The worldly aspects of the Church fundamentally include that many different people work together for the fulfillment of the Church's mission and also require the appropriate material resources for their respective activities. Salaries must be paid, church buildings maintained, parish halls constructed, cooperation coordinated, contracts fulfilled, catechetical material printed—the list goes on and on. But at the end of the day, all of these examples relate to one insight: In order to fulfill all of these tasks that arise from the mission of the Church—and thereby also the mission of the Church itself—there is a need for a fully functional administration, which must be oriented toward the goal of the Church and based on the principle of justice.

Administration standardizes procedures and processes, so that it is not necessary to seek, ask, and try out how something works every time, even though the same things need to be done repeatedly. This conserves resources and uses them sparingly and efficiently for the mission. Administration documents what has been discussed, agreed, and achieved; it prevents forgetfulness and preserves matters beyond the moment, so that reliability and fidelity to one's own word are possible. Administration objectifies by creating and enforcing rules and laws and thus helps prevent arbitrariness. This is an active contribution to justice, since binding rules and laws ensure that decisions and judgments are not merely based on the whims of those carrying them out or of superiors. Administration also orientates and sorts by maintaining an overview of what happens, thereby recording it and making it available. Thus, it creates order, in which the individual can find their way and understand or review the rationale of their own actions. Administration regulates, and it sanctions infringements against the common interest, rules, and laws, and thus acts as a counterweight to what can be commonly described as the sinfulness of humanity. Taken overall, administration stabilizes cooperation between different people in institutions.

All that has been mentioned so far, including standardizing, documenting, objectifying, orientating, and sorting, as well as regulating, is of decisive importance for the success of joint actions, including those of the Church.

Difficulties and problems

On the basis of all this that administration accomplishes, it is powerful. What it does or doesn't do has a significant impact on what can be achieved through joint actions—or not. This power of administration can also be misused. This is the case, for example, if administration forgets its function of serving the different people living together and cooperating to achieve higher goals; if the administration is only preoccupied with itself; if rules and regulations are only used to sustain the administration or the power of persons. This is abuse of power by the administration. What this can mean is clearly apparent at this time.

The sexual abuse of children and youths is in no small measure due to the abuse of power in the area of administration. In this regard, administration has not contributed to fulfilling the mission of the Church, but on the contrary, has obscured, discredited, and made it impossible. Files that could have documented the terrible deeds and named those responsible were destroyed or not even created. Instead of the perpetrators, the victims were regulated and silence imposed on them. The stipulated procedures and processes for the prosecution of offenses were deliberately not complied with, but instead canceled or overridden. The rights of victims were effectively trampled underfoot and left to the whims of individuals. These are all events that sharply contradict what the Church should stand for. The way in which Church administration was structured and carried out did not contribute to unifying the whole human race and bringing mankind closer to God, but on the contrary, violated these aims.

Now, at the very latest, this highlights a difficult dilemma: on the one hand, administration is required to fulfill the mission of the Church, and on the other hand, it can directly oppose this mission. How should this be dealt with? What do we need to change or pay more attention to?

Necessity of traceability and transparency

We urgently need an administration that not only contributes to fulfilling the mission of the Church but to some extent even embodies what should be achieved with this mission. It must—just like the Church as a whole—not only be a tool but also a symbol for the unification of humanity and the unity of mankind with God. It is not only about the functioning of administration for any purpose, but rather that administration should take place in such a way that people feel accepted in administrative procedures, that they feel appreciated, that they can trust the system, that they feel secure and fairly treated, that they are listened to and their legitimate criticism is accepted. This would go a long way toward achieving what it really means to bring people together and ultimately also to bring mankind closer to God—and that is, so to speak, the theological mission of Church administration.

How important it is that Church administration functions in this way is clearly shown by the negative experiences in connection with the cases of abuse. The thoughts of some abuse victims can be summarized as follows: If the Church claims to act in the name of Jesus, yet I am treated so badly by the Church or its administration, then I would also like to have nothing to do with this Jesus.

In order for administration to act in accordance with the Church's mission and with the nature of the Church as a "symbol and instrument," there needs to be transparency and traceability of administrative procedures. Administrative procedures become transparent if it is understandable and traceable who has done what, when, why, and what for, and what has been decided, rejected, or assigned. Thus, people who experience transparent administration can uncover errors and mistakes in the administrative actions and defend themselves against such actions. They can share their perspective in a binding way and have it taken into account. The people encountering the administration are not faced with an anonymous, incomprehensible power structure, but can exercise self-determined control over administrative procedures. They are not mere objects of administration but can perceive themselves instead as subjects. That is why the introduction of administrative jurisdiction in the Church is very appropriate and necessary.

Objections and fears

There are no alternatives to traceability and transparency. However, there are objections that should be considered. They are mainly directed against violations of pontifical secrecy, as well as ruining the reputation of innocent priests or of the priesthood and the Church as a whole through false accusations, if these are spread. These objections to traceability and transparency are not particularly forceful.

Every objection based on pontifical secrecy would only be relevant if compelling reasons could be shown why pontifical secrecy should apply to the prosecution of criminal offenses concerning the abuse of minors. As things stand, I know of no such reasons.

The principles of the presumption of innocence and the protection of personal rights and the need for transparency are not mutually exclusive. The opposite is the case. On the one hand, a transparent, clearly regulated, and defined procedure ensures that the correct steps must be taken before those who should pass judgment actually do so. This is the best safety mechanism against prejudices or false judgments in the matter. On the other hand, a clearly defined and public procedure establishes a degree of credibility, which enables restoring the reputation of a wrongly accused person, who would otherwise be subjected to rumors if the investigation is not appropriate, transparent, or conclusive.

Transparency does not mean the uncritical acceptance and undisciplined dissemination of abuse allegations. The goal is a transparent process, which clarifies and specifies the allegations and follows generally accepted standards regarding when and how the public, the authorities, and the Roman Curia should be informed. Such standard practices will make it clear that it is not transparency that damages the Church but rather the acts of abuse committed, the lack of transparency, or the ensuing cover-up.

Tasks and challenges

Traceability and transparency do not simply appear out of the blue. They are a constant task, whose fulfillment can also be aided by support from relevant experts from outside the Church. What is decisive is always the personal attitude of those who work in administration and those responsible for it. In essence, it is about the question of how far one is willing to justify one's own actions to others and to some extent also be checked by others. Developing such a positive attitude and bringing it to bear in an appropriate manner requires time and space for discussion, differentiation and clarification, and practice and learning. However, in view of the urgency of the topic, the most important measures should be initiated immediately. These may include the following:

1. Definition of the goal and the limits of pontifical secrecy

The social changes of our time are increasingly characterized by changing communication patterns. In the age of social media, in which each and every one of us can almost immediately establish contact and exchange information via Facebook, Twitter, etc., it is necessary to redefine confidentiality and secrecy and to distinguish them from data protection. If we do not succeed, we either squander the chance to maintain a level of self-determination regarding information or we expose ourselves to the suspicion of covering up.

2. Transparent procedural norms and rules for ecclesiastical processes

Court proceedings as legal remedies are meaningless without adequate legal and procedural rules, as this would be tantamount to arbitrariness when it comes to passing judgments. This would represent a lack of transparency in relation to the specific actions. Establishing transparent procedural norms and rules for ecclesiastical processes is essential. The Church must not operate below the quality standards of public administration of justice if it doesn't want to face criticism that it has an inferior legal system, which is harmful to people.

3. Public announcement of statistics on the number of cases, and details thereof, as far as possible

Institutional mistrust leads to conspiracy theories regarding an organization, and the formation of myths about an organization. This can be avoided if the facts are set out transparently.

4. Publication of judicial proceedings

Proper legal proceedings serve to establish the truth and form the basis for imposing a punishment that is appropriate for the relevant offense. In addition, they establish trust in the organization and its leadership. Lingering doubts about the proper conduct of court proceedings only harm the reputation and the functioning of an institution. This principle also applies to the Church.

If one takes a look at the other issues to be dealt with at our meeting, it is clear that traceability and transparency are only one topic among many, to be taken into consideration in connection with abuse prevention and dealing with abuse.

Nevertheless, one should always be aware that traceability and transparency are also extremely important beyond the context of abuse, for example in the area of finances. They are also a decisive factor in the trustworthiness and credibility of the Church. Let us take a courageous step in this direction.

COMMUNICATION:
FOR ALL PEOPLE

Valentina Alazraki, *Journalist and author,*
correspondent for Noticieros Televisa (Mexico)

Introduction

First and foremost, I would like to introduce myself. I am a correspondent in Rome and in the Vatican for *Televisa*, Mexican television. I followed the end of the pontificate of St. Pope Paul VI, the 33 days of the pontificate of John Paul I, the entire pontificates of St. John Paul II, Benedict XVI, and now Pope Francis. I have covered 150 journeys with the latter three Popes.

They invited me to speak to you about communication and, in particular, about how transparent communication is indispensable to fight the sexual abuse of minors by men of the Church.

At first glance, there is little in common between you, bishops and cardinals, and me, a Catholic lay woman with no particular position in the Church, and moreover a journalist. Yet we share something very powerful: we all have a mother; we are here because a woman gave birth to us. Compared to you, perhaps I have an additional privilege: I am first of all a mother.

Therefore, I do not feel that I am a representative just of journalists, but also of mothers, families, civil society. I would like to share with you my experiences and my life and—if you will allow me—to add some practical advice.

My point of departure: motherhood

I would like to begin precisely with motherhood in order to develop the topic entrusted to me, which is: how the Church should communicate about this topic of abuse.

I doubt that anyone in this hall does not think the Church is, first of all, mother. Many of us present here have or have had a brother or sister. Let us also remember that our mothers, while loving us all in the same way, were especially devoted to the frailest, weakest children, to those who perhaps did not know how to move ahead in life on their own feet and needed a little push.

For a mother there are no first- or second-class children; there are stronger children and more vulnerable ones.

Nor are there first- and second-class children for the Church. Her seemingly more important children, as are you, bishops and cardinals (I dare not say the pope), are no more so than any other boy, girl, or young person who has experienced the tragedy of being the victim of abuse by a priest.

What is the Church's mission? To preach the Gospel. But to do so she needs moral authority; coherence between what one preaches and what one lives is the basis of being a credible institution, worthy of trust and respect.

For this reason, in facing criminal conduct such as the abuse of minors, do you think that to be true to herself, an institution like the Church can have another way other than that of reporting this crime? That she can have another way other than that of being on the side of the victim and not that of the oppressor? Who is the weakest, most vulnerable child? The priest who abused, the bishop who abused and covered up, or the victim?

You may be certain that for journalists, mothers, families, and the entire society, the abuse of minors is one of the main causes of anguish. The abuse of minors, the devastation of their lives, of their families' lives, worry us. We believe such abuse is one of the most reprehensible crimes.

Ask yourselves: are you enemies, as determined as we are, of those who commit abuse or who cover them up?

We have decided which side to be on. Have you done so truly, or in word alone?

Allies or enemies

If you are against those who commit or cover up abuse, then we are on the same side. We can be allies, not enemies. We will help you to find the rotten apples and to overcome resistance in order to separate them from the healthy ones.

But if you do not decide in a radical way to be on the side of the children, mothers, families, civil society, you are right to be afraid of us, because we journalists, who seek the common good, will be your worst enemies.

I have been covering the Vatican for almost forty-five years. Five different pontificates, extremely important for the life of the Church and of the world, with lights and shadows. In these four decades I have really seen it all.

How many times have I heard that the scandal of abuse is *the press's fault, that it is a plot by certain media outlets to discredit the Church, that there are hidden powers backing it in order to put an end to this institution!*

We journalists know that there are reporters who are more thorough than others and that there are media outlets more or less dependent on political, ideological, or economic interests. But I believe that in no case can the mass media be blamed for having uncovered or reported on the abuse.

Abuses against minors are neither rumors nor gossip: they are crimes. I remember Pope Benedict XVI's words during the flight to Lisbon, when he told us that the greatest persecution of the Church comes not from external enemies but arises from sins within her.

I would like you to leave this hall with the conviction that we journalist are neither those who abuse nor those who cover up. Our mission is to assert and defend a right, which is a right to information based on truth in order to obtain justice.

We journalists know that abuse is not limited to the Catholic Church, but you must understand that we have to be more rigorous with you than with others, by virtue of your moral role. Stealing, for example, is wrong, but if the one stealing is a police officer it seems more serious to us, because it is the opposite of what he or she should do, which is to protect the community from thieves. If doctors or nurses poison their patients rather than take care of them, the act draws even more of our attention because it goes against their ethics, their professional code.

Lack of communication, another abuse

As a journalist, as a woman and mother, I would like to tell you that we think abusing a minor is as contemptible as is covering up the abuse. And you know better than I that abuses have been covered up systematically, from the ground up.

I think you should be aware that the more you cover up, the more you play ostrich, failing to inform the mass media and thus the faithful and public opinion, the greater the scandal will be. If someone has a tumor, it is not cured by hiding it from one's family or friends; silence will not make it heal. In the end it will be the most suitable treatments that will prevent metastasis and lead to healing.

Communicating is a fundamental duty because, if you fail to do so you automatically become complicit with the abusers. By not providing the information that could prevent these people from committing further abuse, you are not giving the children, young people, and their families the tools to defend themselves against new crimes.

The faithful do not forgive the lack of transparency, because it is a new assault on the victims. Those who fail to inform encourage a climate of suspicion and incite anger and hatred against the institution.

I saw it with my own eyes during Pope Francis' journey to Chile in 2018. There was no indifference; there was indignation and anger for the systematic concealment, for the silence, for the deception of the faithful and the suffering of victims who, for decades, had not been listened to, were not believed.

Victims have first and foremost the right to know what has happened, what you have done in order to distance and punish those who have committed abuse. Even if the guilty party is dead, the victim's pain is not extinguished. Although the guilty party can no longer be punished, at least the victim, who perhaps has lived many years with that hidden wound, can be consoled. Additionally, other victims who remain in silence will dare to come out, and you will promote their healing and their consolation.

Take the initiative

In Spanish we say that he who strikes first lands three strikes. Obviously, it is not a matter of striking but of informing.

I think it would be healthier, more positive, and more helpful if the Church were the first to provide information in a proactive way and not reactive, as normally happens. You should not wait to respond to legitimate questions from the press (or from the people, your people) when a journalistic investigation uncovers a case.

In the age we live in, it is very difficult to hide a secret. With the prominence of social networks, the ease of posting photos, audio, and video, and the rapid social and cultural changes, the Church has only one path: to concentrate on awareness and transparency, which go hand in hand.

Report things when you know them. Of course, it will not be pleasant, but it is the only way, if you want us to believe you when you say "from now on we will no longer tolerate cover-ups." The first to benefit from transparency is the institution, because the focus is on the guilty party.

Learn from past mistakes

I am Mexican and cannot fail to mention perhaps the most terrible case that has happened in the Church, that of Marcial Maciel, the Mexican founder of the Legion of Christ. I witnessed this grim case from beginning to end. Aside from the moral justice over the crimes committed by that man, who according to some was mentally ill and to others an evil genius, I assure you that at the basis of that scandal, which did so much harm to thousands of people, to the point of tarnishing the memory of one who is now a saint, there was unhealthy communication.

One need not forget that in the Legion there was a fourth vow according to which if a member saw something that concerned him regarding a superior, he could not criticize, much less comment about it.

Without this censure, without this total concealment, had there been transparency, Marcial Maciel would not have been able, for decades, to abuse seminarians and to have three or four lives, wives, and children, who came to accuse him of having abused his own children.

For me this is the most emblematic case of unhealthy, corrupt communication, from which various lessons can and must be learned.

Pope Francis told the Curia that in other eras, in addressing these subjects, there was ignorance, lack of preparation, and disbelief. I dare say that there was also corruption.

Behind the silence, the lack of healthy, transparent communication, quite often there is not only the fear of scandal, concern for the institution's good name, but also money, compensation, gifts, construction permits for schools and universities perhaps in areas where construction was not permitted. I am speaking of what I have seen and thoroughly investigated.

Pope Francis always reminds us that the devil enters through the pockets, and he is absolutely right. Transparency will help you to fight economic corruption.

In processing internal information, from the ground up, we have learned even from various nuncios, and I can testify to this, that there have been cases of cover-up, obstacles barring access to the pope of the time, underestimating the gravity of the information or discrediting it, as if it were the fruit of obsessions or fantasies.

Transparency will also help you to fight corruption in the government. It was also thanks to some courageous victims, several courageous journalists, and, I think I must say it, a courageous pope like Benedict XVI, that this scandal was made public and the tumor eradicated.

It is extremely important to learn the lesson and not to repeat the same mistake. Transparency will help you to be coherent with the Gospel message and to put into practice the principle according to which in the Church no one is above the law: we are all accountable to God and to others.

Avoid secrecy, embrace transparency

Secrecy, understood as an excessive tendency to keep secrets, is closely tied to the abuse of power; it is like a safety net for those who abuse power. Today our societies have adopted transparency as a general rule, and the public believes that the only reason not to be transparent is the desire to conceal something negative or corrupt.

My sense is that within the Church there is still more resistance to recognizing that the problem of abuse exists, and it is imperative to address it with all the instruments possible. Some believe that it happens only in certain countries. I believe we can speak of a generalized situation, to a greater or lesser extent, which in any case must be dealt with and resolved.

Those who hide something are not necessarily corrupt, but all corrupt people are hiding something. Not all those who keep secrets are committing an abuse of power, but all those who abuse power are generally hiding things.

Of course, transparency has its limitations. For this reason, we do not expect you to inform us of just any accusation against a priest. We understand that there can and must be a prior investigation, but do so quickly, comply with the laws of the country you live in, and if it's called for, present the case to the civil justice system.

If the accusation is shown to be credible, you must provide information about the ongoing processes, about what you are doing. You must say that you have removed the guilty party from his parish or from where he was practicing. You must report it yourselves, both in the dioceses and in the Vatican. At times, the Bulletin of the Holy See Press Office provides information about a resignation without explaining the reasons. There are priests who have gone immediately to inform the faithful that they were ill and not that they were leaving because they had committed abuse. I think that the news about the resignation of a priest who has committed abuse should be released with clarity, in an explicit way.

In *Camera Caritatis*, silence on these topics is permissible only if it injures no one, but never when it can do harm.

Three practical tips for living transparency

I have already told you that I think communication is indispensable to resolving this problem. Now allow me to suggest three ways for you to put transparency into practice at the moment of communicating about the sexual abuse of minors.

1. Put the victims in first place

If the Church wants to learn how to communicate about abuse, her first point of reference must be the victim. Pope Francis has asked the participants in this meeting to meet the victims, to listen to them, and to be available to them before coming to Rome. I will not ask you to raise your hand to see who has done so, but answer silently to yourselves. Victims are not just numbers; they are not statistics. They are people whose lives, sexuality, emotions, trust in other human beings, perhaps even God, as well as the ability to love, have been ruined.

And why is this important? Because it is difficult to be informed about and communicate something about which we have no direct knowledge.

In the case of abuse, it is even more obvious. We cannot speak about this subject if we have not listened to the victims, if we have not shared their pain, if we have not touched by hand the wounds that abuse has caused not only in their bodies but also in their minds, in their hearts, in their faith. If you meet them, they will have a name; they will have a face, and the experience you have with them will be reflected not only in the way in which you confront the issue, but also in the way in which you communicate and resolve it.

The pope has told us that he meets them regularly, at Santa Marta, that he considers them one of his priorities. You should do the same; I do not believe you have less time than the pope. Remember, transparency is showing what you do. Only if you put the victims in first place will you be credible when you say you have decided to eradicate the scourge of abuse.

2. Seek counsel for yourselves

The second thing is to let yourselves seek advice. Before making decisions, seek advice from people with sound judgment who can help you. There should always be communicators among these advisors. I think the Church should have, at all levels, communications experts and should heed them when they tell her that it is always better to inform than to keep silent or even lie. It is an illusion to think that a scandal can be hidden today. It is like covering the sky with a finger. It cannot be done. It is no longer acceptable or permissible. Thus, all of you must understand that silence is far more costly than facing reality and making it public.

I think it is essential that you invest in communications in all your ecclesiastical structures, with highly qualified and experienced individuals in order to address the demands for transparency in today's world.

The role of the spokesperson is fundamental. Not only must it be a highly trained individual, but he or she must also be able to rely on the full trust of the bishop and have direct access to him twenty-four hours a day. This is not a 9 to 5 job. Anything can happen at any moment, and at any moment there can be a need to react, although, I repeat, it would be better if you were the first to provide the news.

We journalists prefer to speak directly with the boss. But we accept speaking with a spokesperson, if we know that he or she has access to the boss and passes on what the boss, fully apprised, is thinking.

3. Professionalize your communications
In the third place, you must communicate better.

What kind of transparency do journalists, mothers, families, the faithful, public opinion expect from an institution such as the Church? I think it is fundamental that, at every level, from the parish up to here, in the Vatican, there be structures perhaps standardized but very agile and flexible, that quickly offer accurate information. It may be incomplete for lack of a deeper investigation, but the response cannot be silence or "no comment," because then we will seek answers by asking others, and thus it will be third parties informing people in the way they wish to do so.

If you do not have all the necessary information available, if there are doubts, if there is already an investigation, it is better to explain this in the best way possible so as not to give the impression that you do not want to respond because you are hiding something. It is important to follow up on the information at all times, and it is especially important to react quickly. If information is not given in a timely manner, the response is no longer of interest; it will be too late and others will do so, perhaps incorrectly.

The risk is high, and the price of this kind of conduct is even higher. Silence gives the impression that the accusations—be they true or false, partly true and partly false—are totally true and that there is fear of giving a response that can be immediately contradicted.

I have seen with my own eyes how bad information, or inadequate information, has caused tremendous damage, harmed the victims and their families, not allowed justice to be served, caused the faith of many people to waver.

I assure you that investing in communications is a very profitable matter and is not a short-term investment; it is a long-term investment.

Conclusion

I would like to conclude this address by mentioning a different topic than that of the abuse of minors, but important for a woman journalist such as myself.

We are at the threshold of another scandal, that of nuns and women religious as victims of sexual abuse by priests and bishops. *L'Osservatore Romano*'s magazine on women's issues has reported it and, during the return flight from Abu Dhabi, Pope Francis acknowledged that work has been underway on this subject for some time, that it is true that more needs to be done, and that there is a will to do more.

I would like that on this occasion the Church play offense and not defense, as has happened in the case of the abuse of minors. It could be a great opportunity for the Church to take the initiative and be on the forefront of denouncing these abuses, which are not only sexual but also abuses of power.

As I take my leave, I thank Pope Francis for having expressed his gratitude, before the Curia last December, for the work of journalists, who have been honest and objective in uncovering predatory priests and have made victims' voices heard.

I hope that after this meeting you will return home and not avoid us, but instead seek us out. That you will return to your dioceses thinking that we are not vicious wolves, but, on the contrary, that we can join our forces against the real wolves.

Thank you.

SUMMARY OF THE REPORTS
OF THE WORKING GROUPS

Fr. Federico Lombardi, sj, *President of the Joseph Ratzinger-Benedict XVI Foundation, Moderator of the Meeting*

The working groups into which the participants of the meeting were distributed were eleven (four in English, two in French, two in Spanish, three in Italian). The organizers proposed a composition that would facilitate not only the exchange in the preferred language, but also the exchange among people from different regions and cultures. Participants belonging to Eastern churches, to female and male religious congregations were also distributed as much as possible in different groups.

The times in which the groups worked were limited (one hour in the morning and one in the afternoon during the first two days and an hour in the morning on the third day, for a total of five hours), as were the reporting times for the groups in the General Assembly (one hour on each of the first two days, for a total of two hours) but with very rich and punctual reports, although short.

The reports of the working groups were delivered in writing and will represent valuable material for reflection. The Moderator put together a brief summary of the reports that will be part of the official transcripts of the Meeting, as a testimony of the importance of the teams' work within the overall framework of the Meeting. The topics that the groups focused on are briefly outlined.

Break and overcome the "culture of silence"

We realize the severity of the consequences of not listening and recognizing the suffering and depth of the victims' wounds and underestimating and even trying to hide the seriousness of the crimes of child sexual abuse.

The difficulties of overcoming the culture of silence is greater in certain cultures and regions of the world. However, we must commit ourselves to developing a positive "culture of denunciation," which will allow us to act effectively in truth and justice.

We need to understand more deeply the dynamics and processes that lead to abuse and their "systemic" nature; the connections between abuses of power, conscience, and sexuality; the distorted vision of authority in the Church as power and not as a service, identified by Pope Francis as "clericalism."

Attention to the victims

The priority of listening to the victims was reiterated by all groups, where the strength of the testimonies heard was recognized to provide the most adequate understanding of the problems, the severity of the suffering, and the depth of the wounds, and therefore of the severity of the concealment and the negligence of acting to respond to the victims, to do justice and prevent the perpetrators from repeating the crimes.

Often, the victims' deep wounds are caused not only by the abuse itself, but also in large part by the experience of not being listened to. This has often caused deep resentment and has hardened the already critical attitudes. Although it may be difficult, it is right to keep cultivating an attitude of listening to all victims.

To ensure listening, it is necessary to provide specific people and places, familiar with the victims and their families. However, this does not exempt the bishops from also listening in person, which is necessary to understand the nature and depth of the problems. Listening must be a "structural" part of the bishop's pastoral ministry.

It is necessary to develop skills, not only for active listening, but also to accompany victims and wounded persons. One group in particular spoke of the importance of creating paths to healing and reintegration of the victims within the body of the ecclesial community, also with appropriate rites and liturgies, including participation in the Eucharist as a place of full communion in the body of Christ which has been profaned and hurt by abuse.

We can aim to have victims participate in helping other victims and in the journey toward healing and renewal in ecclesial communities.

Furthermore, the need to recognize the victims' greater role during canonical trials has also been discussed.

Renewing relationships in the Church

Collegiality. The Meeting helped to deepen the awareness of the common responsibility of the bishops for the mission of the Church and thus for the response to the crisis caused by the rise of the abuse scandal. The awareness of solidarity among them in helping and supporting each other to face the crisis adequately (the knowledge and exchange of procedures, experiences, and concrete help for those who need it most) has followed at the level of episcopal conferences and dioceses.

Synodality. Everyone recognized the need for the People of God, the ecclesial communities, to walk together to respond to the problems caused by abuses. Emphasis was placed on the importance of the participation and collaboration of the laity—in particular of women—with their specific skills and sensitivity, in the different entities to be set up in support to the bishop (commissions for the evaluation of abuse reports; "independent" commissions for examining and studying all the cases including those from the past; commissions to verify the implementation of procedures and measures taken; commissions for the training activities of seminarians, ecclesial personnel; commissions for activities and initiatives of prevention for families and communities...).

The importance of collaboration between dioceses and religious congregations was discussed, as well as the consistency of the criteria and procedures adopted, even in the field of moving religious personnel from one place to another.

Subsidiarity and the relationship between duties of the bishops and the episcopal conferences was discussed (for example, it is important that the conferences receive an overall picture of the problems, including adequate information from the dioceses to develop common statistics and guidelines and evaluate their implementation), as well as between the episcopal conferences and Rome (evaluating the analysis and the judgment of cases also at decentralized level—national or regional courts—to avoid accumulation in Rome and delays; even having a local phase of information and evaluation of the problems related to negligence or incompetence in the government of bishops).

Encourage the growth of awareness, competence, clarity, and knowledge of procedures.

It turned out that many bishops still do not know with the necessary clarity what their tasks and duties are with regard to the problems of sexual abuse. In fact, one of the goals of the meeting of which the pope spoke was precisely that of helping to achieve this clarity.

Therefore it has been reiterated that not only should the guidelines of the episcopal conferences (already requested years ago by the Congregation for the Doctrine of the Faith and developed by the majority of the Conferences) be drafted, published, implemented, and verified, but also that a handbook for all bishops be developed and published, in which their tasks and duties and the mandatory nature of the rules are clearly stated. The preparation of such a handbook was announced by the Congregation for the Doctrine of the Faith and is very much awaited.

Among other topics were the "codes of conduct" for bishops and priests, as well as the demands of correct diocesan "administration" (following precise procedures and keeping adequate documentation in the archives; see report by Card. Marx). All this is important to effectively proceed in the direction of "accountability" in our responsibilities and evaluating the way in which management duties have been exercised.

Regarding the evaluation of administration by bishops and superiors, the importance of deepening and clarifying the procedures and methods of application of the motu proprio *As a Loving Mother* on behalf of the Roman dicasteries involved was discussed, as well as the proposals on the phase of information and evaluation at the local level (on the possible role of the Metropolitan, on the collaboration of groups of experts that include lay people; see Cardinal Cupich's report).

The collaboration of the laity and in particular of women

Much has been said about it in the context of the synodality of the Church and the various forms in which the bishop and the episcopal conferences absolutely need competent collaboration to face the different dimensions of the problems (listening to the victims; listening to and evaluating reports and accusations; accompaniment of victims and offenders; prevention in different areas: family, parish community, school, pastoral activities; formation of clergy and ecclesial personnel…).

Competent lay people, including women, can also have a larger role even in ecclesiastical courts. Needless to say, this participation at a professional level also will require fair remuneration.

The specific importance of female participation was often noted by the working groups, and it must grow. We insist on its importance in the phases of listening and accompaniment (many victims, especially women, certainly prefer to open up to other women), of prevention (in some regions, the people who are most available and capable of training and commitment to child protection are religious people), etc.

Formation of the clergy

In some groups there has been in-depth discussion of the problems and usefulness of the "minor seminaries," criticized in one of the reports.

In all the groups, the urgency of improvement of the human, affective, and integral formation of the candidates to the priesthood was reiterated, also in the dimension of sexuality. The importance of the presence of women in the course of formation, of having people with psychological skills, of the use of psychological tests was appreciated, in order to avoid the acceptance of people unsuitable to the sacred orders.

The problem of "clericalism," that is, a mistaken vision of authority in the Church and a privileged and superior place of the clergy toward the faithful, must be faced with determination starting with the seminary formation.

The importance of information among bishops or competent superiors about seminarians or priests who transfer from one seminary to another or from one diocese to another was insisted upon.

The importance of the formation of seminarians was also highlighted with regard to the digital world, since the risk of dependence on pornography is also present among seminarians and the clergy.

A proposal was also made to require a clear and formal personal statement of one's commitment to avoid sexual abuse (as required for celibacy) before ordination.

The continuing formation and the accompaniment of the clergy, especially of the young clergy, is very important. In this sense, spiritual life must be treated in the context of celibacy, which is certainly not directly linked to abuse but can be connected to a risk of withdrawal in solitude rather than of an integrated and balanced development of personality.

We also need to recognize that the great majority of the clergy faithfully carries out their ministry, and we must support it and encourage it in this time of painful trial, because the grave infidelity of some is casting a shadow over the credibility of all.

In several groups the existence of a relationship between sexual abuse and homosexuality was discussed among us. The issue is complex and for various reasons it can be assumed that there is no connection. However, the matter deserves further study in regard to the Catholic clergy, since the majority of known abuse cases by members of the clergy affected boys rather than girls.

A proposal suggested by one group concerns the formation of bishops in the area of child protection, both on the occasion of trainings for the new bishops and on the occasion of the five-year *ad limina* visits, and with more in-depth special training weeks on the topic.

The offenders

Several groups discussed how to deal with offenders. Appropriate psychological and psychiatric therapies were discussed, as well as spiritual accompaniment and the duty of not abandoning these people. It is a matter of reconciling the demands of justice and mercy. It should not be forgotten that in several cases the abusers had been victims in the past.

We talked about "zero tolerance," of the meaning of this phrase and of its interpretation and implementation by some important episcopal conferences: to face all cases with rigor and without exceptions and to exclude from public ministry the people found guilty of abuse. However, there was also talk of the different interpretations that this term receives, of its legal vagueness, and the difficulty of seeing it compatible with the principle of proportionality of the sentence; not to mention that it does not sound evangelical.

The issue of the term "credible accusations" before the actual ruling was also addressed, as well as the publication of lists of accused priests and how this is incompatible with the "presumption of innocence." We need to be aware that often an accusation is enough, without a conviction that follows, to irreparably destroy the reputation and the real possibility of reintegration into the ecclesial life of a priest.

Transparency

Transparency means first of all the publication and knowledge of the rules and procedures that must be followed, following them effectively, and being able to verify behaviors, actions, and results.

Additionally, it means having data and information useful to understand problems. In this regard, reliable statistics that can be correctly interpreted are desired. More detailed reports on the situation would be desired.

If there has been a final sentence of conviction, it is just that it be shared, and the reasons for a bishop's dismissal from his role should be known as well. On the other hand, the publication of names of accused people who have not yet been convicted is problematic, unless it is requested for reasons of the common good or it is not made necessary by the circumstances.

It must not be forgotten that transparency must be an attitude that characterizes all communication within and on behalf of the Church, not only in regard to sexual abuse, but also to the economy, etc.

It is necessary to clarify the topic of the "secret": pontifical secret, confidentiality of investigations, the seal of office, professional secrecy, seal of the confessional. The elimination of the "pontifical secret" in connection with the proceedings on sexual abuse of minors has been mentioned often, but we need to explain what it entails.

Furthermore, it is good that transparency and communication are carried out in a positive way, by letting people know how much is being done in the field of child protection and prevention.

In collaboration with civil authorities, access must be given to requested documents, but only to those documents concerning specific, investigated cases and not an indiscriminate access to all.

Diverse cultural situations

As far as Africa is concerned, we found out about the difficulty of overcoming a negative culture of silence on sexuality and abuse, as well as the tradition of dealing with problems within the extended family and community. This should also be considered in regard to our topic.

In groups where people come from predominantly Muslim countries, it has been enormously difficult or impossible to bring to light and deal with sexual abuse issues based on current criteria of other regions of the world.

Similarly, in predominantly Orthodox Christian countries there is great resistance to addressing these problems, and the Catholic Church is impacted while doing its utmost to increase awareness and responsibility.

In former Communist countries, we noticed that the use of the word "clericalism" has historically been associated with the struggle of oppressive regimes to fight and destroy the Church; it must therefore be used with caution.

Hope

In several groups it has been observed that the situation of trial and crisis must be lived as an opportunity for purification and growth of the community of the Church. It is a call to a profound renewal.

We must bring to the center positive attention on children and minors as an essential dimension of the mission of the Church.

PENANCE SERVICE

TESTIMONIAL OF A VICTIM
OF SEXUAL ABUSE

Abuse of any kind is the worst humiliation which an individual can experience. One is confronted with the fact of having to recognize that one cannot—and may not—defend oneself against the superior strength of the offender. You cannot escape what happens, but must endure it, no matter what or how bad it is. When experiencing abuse, one would like to end it all. But this is not possible.

One wants to flee, and so it comes to pass that you are no longer yourself. One tries to flee, by effectively trying to flee oneself. Thus, with time, one becomes completely alone. You are alone, because you have retreated elsewhere, and you can't/don't want to return to yourself. The more often it happens, the less you return to yourself. You are someone else, and will always remain so. What you carry inside you is like a ghost, which others are unable to see. They will never fully see and know you. What hurts the most is the certainty that nobody will understand you. That lives with you, for the rest of your life.

The attempts to return to the own true self and participate in the "previous" world, as it was before the abuse, are just as painful as the abuse itself. One always lives in these two worlds simultaneously. I wish that the perpetrators could understand that they create this split in the victim. For the rest of our lives.

The greater your desire and your efforts to reconcile these two worlds, the more painful the certainty that this is not possible. There is no dream without memories of what has occurred, no day without flashbacks.

I now manage to cope with this better, by learning to live with these two lives. I try to focus on the God-given right to be allowed to live. I can and should be here. This gives me courage. It's over now. I can now go on. I should continue. If I give up now or stand still, I will allow the injustice to interfere with my life. I can prevent this by learning to control it and by learning to speak about it.

HOMILY

Archbishop Philip Naameh, *Archbishop of Tamale,*
President of the Episcopal Conference of Ghana

Dear brothers and sisters,

The Gospel of the prodigal son is well known to us. We have often recounted it and often preached about it. It is almost taken for granted in our congregations and communities, to address the sinners and to encourage them to repent. We perhaps already do this so routinely that we forget something important. We readily forget to apply this Scripture to ourselves, to see ourselves as we are, namely as prodigal sons.

Just like the prodigal son in the Gospel, we have also demanded our inheritance, got it, and now we are busy squandering it. The current abuse crisis is an expression of this. The Lord has entrusted us with the management of the goods of salvation. He trusts that we will fulfill his mission, proclaim the Good News, and help to establish the kingdom of God. But what do we do? Do we do justice to what is entrusted to us? We will not be able to answer this question with a sincere yes, beyond all doubts. Too often we have kept quiet, looked the other way, avoided conflicts. We were too smug to confront ourselves with the dark sides of our Church. We have thereby squandered the trust placed in us, especially with regard to abuse within the area of responsibility of the Church, which is primarily our responsibility. We have not afforded people the protection they are entitled to, have destroyed hopes, and people were massively violated in both body and soul.

The prodigal son in the Gospel loses everything—not only his inheritance, but also his social status, his good standing, his reputation. We should not be surprised if we suffer a similar fate, if people talk badly about us, if there is distrust toward us, if some threaten to withdraw their material support. We should not complain about this, but instead ask what we should do differently. No one can exempt themselves, nobody can say: but I have personally not done anything wrong. We are a brotherhood, we bear responsibility not only for ourselves, but also for every other member of our brotherhood, and for the brotherhood as a whole.

What must we do differently, and where should we start? Let us look again at the prodigal son in the Gospel. For him, the situation starts to take a turn for the better when he decides to be very humble, to perform very simple tasks, and not to demand any privileges. His situation changes as he recognizes himself, admits to having made a mistake, confesses this to his father, speaks openly about it, and is ready to accept the consequences. In this way, the Father experiences great joy at the return of his prodigal son and facilitates the brothers' mutual acceptance.

Can we also do this? Are we willing to do so? The current meeting will reveal this, must reveal this, if we want to show that we are worthy sons of the Lord, our Heavenly Father. As we have heard and discussed today and the previous two days, this includes taking responsibility, demonstrating accountability, and establishing transparency.

There is a long road ahead of us, to actually implement all of this sustainably in an appropriate manner. We have made different progress and attained different speeds. The current meeting was only one step of many. We should not believe that just because we have begun to change something together, that all difficulties have thereby been eliminated. As with the son who returns home in the Gospel, everything is not yet accomplished; at the very least, he must still win over his brother again. We should also do the same: win over our brothers and sisters in the congregations and communities, regain their trust, and re-establish their willingness to cooperate with us, to contribute to establishing the kingdom of God.

Conclusion

EUCHARISTIC CELEBRATION

(1 Samuel 26:2, 7–9, 12–13, 22–23; 1 Corinthians 15:45–49;
Luke 6:27–38)

Homily

ARCHBISHOP MARK BENEDICT COLERIDGE, *Archbishop of Brisbane, President of the Episcopal Conference of Australia*

In the Gospel just proclaimed, one voice alone is heard, the voice of Jesus. Earlier we heard the voice of Paul and at the end of Mass we will hear the voice of Peter, but in the Gospel there is only the voice of Jesus. It is good that, after all our words, there are now only the words of Christ: Jesus alone remains, as on the mount of the Transfiguration (cf. Luke 9:36).

He speaks to us of power, and he does so in this splendid Sala Regia, which also speaks of power. Here are images of battles, of a religious massacre, of struggles between emperors and popes. This is a place where earthly and heavenly powers meet, touched at times by infernal powers as well. In this Sala Regia, the word of God invites us to contemplate power, as we have done through these days together. Between meeting, Sala, and Scripture, therefore, we have a fine harmony of voices.

Standing over the sleeping Saul, David appears a powerful figure, as Abishai sees only too well: "Today God has put the enemy into your hands. So let me nail him to the ground with the spear." But David retorts, "Don't kill him! Who has ever laid a hand on the Lord's consecrated one and gone unpunished?" David chooses to use power not to destroy but to save the king, the Lord's anointed.

The pastors of the Church, like David, have received a gift of power—

power, however, to serve, to create; a power that is with and for, but not over; a power, as St. Paul says, "which the Lord gave for building you up, not for destroying you" (2 Corinthians 10:8). Power is dangerous, because it can destroy; and in these days we have pondered how in the Church, power can turn destructive when separated from service, when it is not a way of loving, when it becomes power *over*.

A host of the Lord's consecrated ones have been placed in our hands—and by the Lord himself. Yet we can use this power not to create but to destroy, and even in the end to kill. In sexual abuse, the powerful lay hands on the Lord's consecrated ones, even the weakest and most vulnerable of them. They say yes to the urging of Abishai, and they seize the spear.

In abuse and its concealment, the powerful show themselves not men of heaven but men of earth, in the words of St. Paul we have heard. In the Gospel, the Lord commands, "Love your enemies." But who is the enemy? Surely not those who have challenged the Church to see abuse and its concealment for what they really are, above all the victims and survivors who have led us to the painful truth by telling their stories with such courage. At times, however, we have seen victims and survivors as the enemy, but we have not loved them, we have not blessed them. In that sense, we have been our own worst enemy.

The Lord urges us to "be merciful as your Father is merciful." Yet, for all that we desire a truly safe Church and for all that we have done to ensure it, we have not always chosen the mercy of the man of heaven. We have, at times, preferred instead the indifference of the man of earth and the desire to protect the Church's reputation and even our own. We have shown too little mercy, and therefore we will receive the same, because the measure we give will be the measure we receive in return. We will not go unpunished, as David says, and we have already known punishment.

The man of earth must die so that the man of heaven can be born; the old Adam must give way to the new Adam. This will require a true conversion, without which we will remain on the level of "mere adminis-tration"—as the Holy Father writes in *Evangelii Gaudium*—"mere admin-istration" which leaves untouched the heart of the abuse crisis (n. 25).

This conversion alone will enable us to see that the wounds of those who have been abused are our wounds, that their fate is our fate, that they are not our enemies but bone of our bones, flesh of our flesh (cf. Genesis 2:23). They are us, and we are them.

This conversion is in fact a Copernican revolution. Copernicus proved that the sun does not revolve around the earth but the earth around the sun. For us, the Copernican revolution is the discovery that those who have been abused do not revolve around the Church but the Church around them. In discovering this, we can begin to see with their eyes and to hear with their ears; and once we do that, the world and the Church begin to look very different. This is the necessary conversion, the true revolution, and the great grace that can open for the Church a new season of mission.

Lord, when did we see you abused and did not come to help you? But he will reply: In truth I say to you, as often as you failed to do this to one of these the least of my brothers and sisters, you failed to do it to me (cf. Matthew 25:44–45). In them, the least of the brothers and sisters, victims and survivors, we encounter Christ crucified, the powerless one from whom there flows the power of the Almighty, the powerless one around whom the Church revolves forever, the powerless one whose scars shine like the sun.

In these days we have been on Calvary—even in the Vatican and in the Sala Regia we are on the dark mountain. In listening to survivors, we have heard Christ crying out in the darkness (cf. Mark 15:34). And the cry has even become music. But here hope is born from his wounded heart, and hope becomes prayer, as the universal Church gathers around us in this upper room: may the darkness of Calvary lead the Church throughout the world to the light of Easter, to the Lamb who is the sun that never sets (cf. Revelation 21:23).

In the end, there remains only the voice of the Risen Lord, urging us not to stand gazing at the empty tomb, wondering in our perplexity what to do next. Nor can we stay in the upper room where he says, "Peace be with you" (John 20:19). He breathes on us (cf. John 20:22) and the fire of a new Pentecost touches us (cf. Acts 2:2). He who is peace throws open the doors of the upper room and the doors of our heart. From fear is born an apostolic boldness, from deep discouragement the joy of the Gospel. A mission stretches before us—a mission demanding not just words but real, concrete action.

We will do all we can to bring justice and healing to survivors of abuse; we will listen to them, believe them, and walk with them; we will ensure that those who have abused are never again able to offend; we will call to account those who have concealed abuse; we will strengthen the processes of recruitment and formation of Church leaders; we will educate all our people in what safeguarding requires; we will do all in our power to make sure that the horrors of the past are not repeated and that the Church is a safe place for all, a loving mother especially for the young and the vulnerable; we will not act alone but will work with all concerned for the good of the young and the vulnerable; we will continue to deepen our own understanding of abuse and its effects, of why it has happened in the Church, and what must be done to eradicate it. All of this will take time, but we do not have forever, and we dare not fail.

If we can do this and more, we will not only know the peace of the Risen Lord, but we will become his peace in a mission to the ends of the earth. Yet we will become the peace only if we become the sacrifice. To this we say yes with one voice as at the altar we plunge our failures and betrayals, all our faith, our hope, our love into the one sacrifice of Jesus, Victim and Victor, who "will wipe away the tears from every eye, and death shall be no more, neither shall there be mourning or weeping or pain any more, for the former things have passed away" (Revelation 21:4).

CONCLUDING ADDRESS OF
HIS HOLINESS POPE FRANCIS

Dear Brothers and Sisters,

As I thank the Lord who has accompanied us during these days, I would like to thank all of you for the ecclesial spirit and concrete commitment that you have so generously demonstrated.

Our work has made us realize once again that the gravity of the scourge of the sexual abuse of minors is, and historically has been, a widespread phenomenon in all cultures and societies. Only in relatively recent times has it become the subject of systematic research, thanks to changes in public opinion regarding a problem that was previously considered taboo; everyone knew of its presence, yet no one spoke of it. I am reminded too of the cruel religious practice, once widespread in certain cultures, of sacrificing human beings—frequently children—in pagan rites. Yet even today, the statistics available on the sexual abuse of minors drawn up by various national and international organizations and agencies (the WHO, UNICEF, INTERPOL, EUROPOL, and others) do not represent the real extent of the phenomenon, which is often underestimated, mainly because many cases of the sexual abuse of minors go unreported,[1] particularly the great number committed within families.

Rarely, in fact, do victims speak out and seek help.[2] Behind this reluctance there can be shame, confusion, fear of reprisal, various forms of guilt, distrust of institutions, forms of cultural and social conditioning, but also lack of information about services and facilities that can help. Anguish tragically leads to bitterness, even suicide, or at times to seek

---

1   Cf. Maria Isabel Martínez Pérez, *Abusos sexuales en niños y adolescentes*, ed. Criminología y Justicia, 2012, according to which only 2% of cases are reported, especially when the abuse has taken place in the home. She sets the number of victims of pedophilia in our society at between 15% and 20%. Only 50% of children reveal the abuses they have suffered, and of these cases only 15% are actually reported. Only 5% end up going to trial.

2   One out of three mentions the fact to no one (2017 data compiled by the non-profit organization THORN).

revenge by doing the same thing. The one thing certain is that millions of children in the world are victims of exploitation and of sexual abuse.

It would be important here to cite the overall data—in my opinion, still partial—on the global level,[3] then from Europe, Asia, the Americas, Africa, and Oceania, in order to give an idea of the gravity and the extent

---

3   *On the global level*: in 2017, the World Health Organization estimated that up to 1 billion minors between 2 and 17 years of age have experienced acts of violence or physical, emotional, or sexual neglect. Sexual abuse (ranging from groping to rape), according to some 2014 UNICEF estimates, would affect 120 million girls, who are the greatest number of victims. In 2017, UNICEF reported that in 38 of the world's low to middle income countries, almost 17 million adult women admitted having had a forced sexual relation in childhood.

Europe: in 2013, the World Health Organization estimated over 18 million abuses. According to UNICEF, in 28 European countries, about 2.5 million young women reported having experienced sexual abuse with or without physical contact prior to 15 years of age (data released in 2017). In addition, 44 million (equivalent to 22.9%) were victims of physical violence, while 55 million (29.6%) were victims of psychological violence. Not only this: in 2017, the INTERPOL Report on the sexual exploitation of minors led to the identification of 14,289 victims in 54 European countries. With regard to Italy, in 2017 CESVI estimated that 6 million children experienced mistreatment. Furthermore, according to data provided by *Telefono Azzurro*, in the calendar year 2017, 98 cases of sexual abuse and pedophilia were handled by the *Servizio 114 Emergenza Infanzia*, equivalent to about 7.5% of the total cases handled by that service. 65% of the minors seeking help were female victims and over 40% were under 11 years of age.

Asia: in India, in the decade 2001-2011, the Asian Centre for Human Rights reported a total of 48,338 cases of the rape of minors, with an increase equivalent to 336% over that period: the 2,113 cases in 2001 rose to 7,112 cases in 2011.

The Americas: in the United States, official government data state that more than 700,000 children each year are victims of violence and mistreatment. According to the International Centre for Missing and Exploited Children (ICMEC), 1 out of every 10 children experiences sexual abuse.

Africa: in South Africa, the results of a study conducted by the Centre for Justice and Crime Prevention of the University of Cape Town showed in 2016 that 1 out of 3 South African young people, male or female, risks being sexually abused before the age of 17. According to the study, the first of its kind on a national scale in South Africa, 784,967 young people between 15 and 17 years of age have already experienced sexual abuse. The victims in this case are for the most part male youths. Not even a third of them reported the violence to the authorities. In other African countries, cases of sexual abuse of minors are part of the wider context of acts of violence linked to the conflicts affecting the continent and are thus difficult to quantify. The phenomenon is also closely linked to the widespread practice of underage marriages in various African nations, as elsewhere.

Oceania: in Australia, according to data issued by the Australian Institute of Health and Welfare (AIHW) in February 2018 and covering the years 2015-2017, one out of six women (16%, i.e., 1.5 million) reported experiencing physical and/or sexual abuse prior to 15 years of age, and one out of nine men (11%, i.e., 992,000) reported having experienced this abuse when they were children. Also, in 2015-2016, around 450,000 children were the object of child protection measures, and 55,600 minors were removed from their homes in order to remedy abuses they had suffered and to prevent others. Finally, one must not forget the risks to which native minors are exposed: again, according to AIHW, in 2015-2016 indigenous children had a seven times greater probability of being abused or abandoned as compared with their non-indigenous contemporaries (cf. http://www.pbc2019.org/protection-of-minors/child-abuse-on-the-global-level).

of this plague in our societies.[4] To avoid needless quibbling, I would point out from the start that the mention of specific countries is purely for the sake of citing the statistical data provided by the aforementioned reports.

The first truth that emerges from the data at hand is that those who perpetrate abuse, that is acts of physical, sexual, or emotional violence, are primarily *parents, relatives, husbands of child brides, coaches, and teachers*. Furthermore, according to the UNICEF data of 2017 regarding twenty-eight countries throughout the world, nine out of every ten girls who have had forced sexual relations reveal that they were victims of someone they knew or who was close to their family.

According to official data of the American government, in the United States over 700,000 children each year are victims of acts of violence and mistreatment. According to the International Centre for Missing and Exploited Children (ICMEC), one out of every ten children experiences sexual abuse. In Europe, 18 million children are victims of sexual abuse.[5] If we take *Italy* as an example, the 2016 *Telefono Azzurro Report* states that 68.9% of abuses take place within the *home* of the minor.[6]

Acts of violence take place not only in the home, but also in neighborhoods, schools, athletic facilities[7] and, sadly, also in church settings.

Research conducted in recent years on the phenomenon of the sexual abuse of minors also shows that the development of the web and of the communications media have contributed to a significant increase in cases of abuse and acts of violence perpetrated online. Pornography is rapidly spreading worldwide through the net. The scourge of pornography has

---

4   The data provided refer to sample counties selected on the basis of the reliability of available sources. The studies released by UNICEF on thirty countries confirm this fact: a small percentage of victims stated that they had asked for help.

5   Cf. https://www.repubblica.it/salute/prevenzione/2016/05/12/news/maltrattamenti_sui_minori_tutti_gli_abusi-139630223.

6   Specifically, those allegedly responsible for the difficulties experienced by a minor are, in 73.7% of the cases a parent (the mother in 44.2% and the father in 29.5%), a relative (3.3%), a friend (3.2%), an acquaintance (3%), a teacher (2.5%). The data show that only in a small percentage of cases (2.2%) is the person responsible an adult stranger. Cf. ibid.

7   A 2011 English study carried out by the National Society for the Prevention of Cruelty to Children (NSPCC) found that 29% of those interviewed reported that they had experienced sexual molestation (physical and verbal) in sports centers.

expanded to an alarming degree, causing psychological harm and damaging relations between men and women, and between adults and children. It is a phenomenon in constant growth. Tragically, a considerable part of pornographic production has to do with minors, who are thus gravely violated in their dignity. The studies in this field—it is sad—document that it is happening in ever more horrible and violent ways, even to the point of acts of abuse against minors being commissioned and viewed live over the net.[8]

Here I would mention the World Congress held in Rome on the theme of child dignity in the digital era, as well as the first Forum of the Interfaith Alliance for Safer Communities held on the same theme in Abu Dhabi last November.

Another scourge is *sexual tourism*. According to 2017 data provided by the World Tourism Organization, each year *three million people* throughout the world travel in order to have sexual relations with a minor.[9] Significantly, the perpetrators of these crimes in most cases do not even realize that they are committing a criminal offence.

We are thus facing a universal problem, tragically present almost everywhere and affecting everyone. Yet we need to be clear, that while gravely affecting our societies as a whole,[10] this evil is in no way less monstrous when it takes place within the Church.

---

8   According to the 2017 data of the Internet Watch Foundation (IWF), every seven minutes a web page sends pictures of sexually abused children. In 2017, 78,589 URLs were found to contain images of sexual abuse concentrated particularly in the Low Countries, followed by the United States, Canada, France and Russia. 55% of the victims were under ten years of age, 86% were girls, 7% boys and 5% both.

9   The most frequented destinations are Brazil, the Dominican Republic, Colombia, as well as Thailand and Cambodia. These have recently been joined by some countries of Africa and Eastern Europe. On the other hand, the six countries from which the perpetrators of abuse mostly come are France, Germany, the United Kingdom, China, Japan and Italy. Not to be overlooked is the growing number of women who travel to developing countries in search of paid sex with minors: in total, they represent 10% of sexual tourists worldwide. Furthermore, according to a study by ECPAT (End Child Prostitution in Asian Tourism) International, between 2015 and 2016, 35% of paedophile sexual tourists were regular clients, while 65% were occasional clients (cf. https://www.osservatoriodiritti.it/2018/03/27/turismo-sessuale-minorile-nel-mondo-italia-ecpat).

10   "For if this grave tragedy has involved some consecrated ministers, we may ask how deeply rooted it may be in our societies and in our families" (Address to the Roman Curia, 21 December 2018).

The brutality of this worldwide phenomenon becomes all the more grave and scandalous in the Church, for it is utterly incompatible with her moral authority and ethical credibility. Consecrated persons, chosen by God to guide souls to salvation, let themselves be dominated by their human frailty or sickness and thus become tools of Satan. In abuse, we see the hand of the evil that does not spare even the innocence of children. No explanations suffice for these abuses involving children. We need to recognize with humility and courage that we stand face to face with the mystery of evil, which strikes most violently against the most vulnerable, for they are an image of Jesus. For this reason, the Church has now become increasingly aware of the need not only to curb the gravest cases of abuse by disciplinary measures and civil and canonical processes, but also to decisively confront the phenomenon both inside and outside the Church. She feels called to combat this evil that strikes at the very heart of her mission, which is to preach the Gospel to the little ones and to protect them from ravenous wolves.

Here again I would state clearly: if in the Church there should emerge even a single case of abuse—which already in itself represents an atrocity—that case will be faced with the utmost seriousness. Brothers and Sisters: in people's justified anger, the Church sees the reflection of the wrath of God, betrayed and insulted by these deceitful consecrated persons. The echo of the silent cry of the little ones who, instead of finding in them fathers and spiritual guides encountered tormentors, will shake hearts dulled by hypocrisy and by power. It is our duty to pay close heed to this silent, choked cry.

It is difficult to grasp the phenomenon of the sexual abuse of minors without considering power, since it is always the result of an abuse of power, an exploitation of the inferiority and vulnerability of the abused, which makes possible the manipulation of their conscience and of their psychological and physical weakness. The abuse of power is likewise present in the other forms of abuse affecting almost 85,000,000 children, forgotten by everyone: child soldiers, child prostitutes, starving children, children kidnapped and often victimized by the horrid commerce of human organs or enslaved, child victims of war, refugee children, aborted children, and so many others.

Before all this cruelty, all this idolatrous sacrifice of children to the god of power, money, pride, and arrogance, empirical explanations alone are not sufficient. They fail to make us grasp the breadth and depth of this tragedy. Here once again we see the limitations of a purely positivistic approach. It can provide us with a true *explanation* that can help us to take necessary measures, but it is incapable of giving us a *meaning*. Today we need both *explanation* and *meaning*. Explanation will help us greatly in the operative sphere, but will take us only halfway.

So what would be the existential *meaning* of this criminal phenomenon? In the light of its human breadth and depth, it is none other than the present-day manifestation of the spirit of evil. If we fail to take account of this dimension, we will remain far from the truth and lack real solutions.

Brothers and sisters, today we find ourselves before a manifestation of brazen, aggressive, and destructive evil. Behind and within, there is the spirit of evil, which in its pride and in its arrogance considers itself the Lord of the world[11] and thinks that it has triumphed. I would like to say this to you with the authority of a brother and a father, certainly a small one and a sinner, but who is the pastor of the Church that presides in charity: in these painful cases, I see the hand of evil that does not spare even the innocence of the little ones. And this leads me to think of the example of Herod who, driven by fear of losing his power, ordered the slaughter of all the children of Bethlehem.[12] Behind this there is Satan.

Just as we must take every practical measure that common sense, the sciences, and society offer us, neither must we lose sight of this reality; we need to take up the spiritual means that the Lord himself teaches us: humiliation, self-accusation, prayer, and penance. This is the only way to overcome the spirit of evil. It is how Jesus himself overcame it.[13]

---

11   Cf. Robert Hugh Benson, *The Lord of the World* (London: Dodd, Mead and Company, 1907).

12   "Quare times, Herodes, quia audis Regem natum? Non venit ille ut te excludat, sed ut diabolum vincat. Sed tu haec non intelligens turbaris et saevis; et ut perdas unum quem quaeris, per tot infantium mortes efficeris crudelis...Necas parvulos corpore quia te necat timor in corde" (SAINT QUODVULTDEUS, *Sermo 2 de Symbolo*: PL 40, 655).

13   "Quemadmodum enim ille, effuso in scientiae lignum veneno suo, naturam gusto corruperat, sic et ipse dominicam carnem vorandam praesumens, deitatis in ea virtute corruptus interituque sublatus est" (SAINT MAXIMUS THE CONFESSOR, *Centuria* 1, 8-3: PG 90, 1182-1186)

The Church's aim will thus be to hear, watch over, protect, and care for abused, exploited, and forgotten children, wherever they are. To achieve that goal, the Church must rise above the ideological disputes and journalistic practices that often exploit, for various interests, the very tragedy experienced by the little ones.

The time has come, then, to work together to eradicate this evil from the body of our humanity by adopting every necessary measure already in force on the international level and ecclesial levels. The time has come to find a correct equilibrium of all values in play and to provide uniform directives for the Church, avoiding the two extremes of a *"justicialism"* provoked by guilt for past errors and media pressure, and a *defensiveness* that fails to confront the causes and effects of these grave crimes.

In this context, I would mention the "best practices" formulated under the guidance of the World Health Organization by a group of ten international bodies[14] that developed and approved a packet of measures called *INSPIRE: Seven Strategies for Ending Violence against Children.*[15]

With the help of these guidelines, the work carried out in recent years by the Pontifical Commission for the Protection of Minors and the contributions made by this Meeting, the Church, in developing her legislation, will concentrate on the following aspects:

---

14   (CDC: United States Centers for Disease Control and Prevention; CRC: Convention on the Rights of the Child; End Violence Against Children: The Global Partnership; PAHO: Pan American Health Organization; PEPFAR: President's Emergency Program for AIDS Relief; TfG: Together for Girls; UNICEF: United Nations Children's Fund; UNODC: United Nations Office on Drugs and Crime; USAID: United States Agency for International Development; WHO: World Health Organization).

15   Each letter of the word *INSPIRE* represents one of the strategies, and for the most part has shown to be preventively effectual against various types of violence, in addition to having benefits in areas such as mental health, education and the reduction of crime. The seven strategies are the following: *Implementation and Enforcement of Laws* (for example, avoiding violent discipline and limiting access to alcohol and firearms); *Norms and Values* that need changing (for example, those that condone sexual abuse against girls or aggressive behavior among boys); *Safe Environments* (for example, identifying neighborhood violence "hot spots" and dealing with local causes through policies that resolve problems and through other interventions); *Parent and Caregiver Support* (for example, by providing formation to parents for their children, and to new parents); *Income and Economic Strengthening* (such as microcredit and formation concerning equity in general); *Response and Support Services* (for example, ensuring that children exposed to violence can have access to effective emergency care and can receive adequate psychosocial support); *Education and Life Skills* (for example, ensuring that children attend school and equipping them with social skills).

1. The protection of children. The primary goal of every measure must be to protect the little ones and prevent them from falling victim to any form of psychological and physical abuse. Consequently, a change of mentality is needed to combat a defensive and reactive approach to protecting the institution and to pursue, wholeheartedly and decisively, the good of the community by giving priority to the victims of abuse in every sense. We must keep ever before us the innocent faces of the little ones, remembering the words of the Master: "Whoever causes one of these little ones who believe in me to sin, it would be better for him to have a great millstone fastened around his neck and to be drowned in the depth of the sea. Woe to the world because of scandals! For it is necessary that scandals come, but woe to the man by whom the scandal comes!" (Matthew 18:6–7).

2. Impeccable seriousness. Here I would reaffirm that "the Church will spare no effort to do all that is necessary to bring to justice whosoever has committed such crimes. The Church will never seek to hush up or not take seriously any case" (Address to the Roman Curia, 21 December 2018). She is convinced that "the sins and crimes of consecrated persons are further tainted by infidelity and shame; they disfigure the countenance of the Church and undermine her credibility. The Church herself, with her faithful children, is also a victim of these acts of infidelity and these real sins of 'peculation'" (ibid.).

3. Genuine purification. Notwithstanding the measures already taken and the progress made in the area of preventing abuse, there is need for a constantly renewed commitment to the holiness of pastors, whose conformity to Christ the Good Shepherd is a right of the People of God. The Church thus restates "her firm resolve to pursue unstintingly a path of purification, questioning how best to protect children, to avoid these tragedies, to bring healing and restoration to the victims, and to improve the training imparted in seminaries....An effort will be made to make past mistakes opportunities for eliminating this scourge, not only from the body of the Church but also from that of society" (ibid.). The holy fear of God leads us to accuse ourselves—as individuals and as an insti tution—and to make up for our failures. Self-accusation is the beginning of wisdom and bound to the holy fear of God: learning how to accuse ourselves, as individuals, as institutions, as a society. For we must not fall into the trap of blaming others, which is a step toward the "alibi" that separates us from reality.

4. Formation. In other words, requiring criteria for the selection and training of candidates to the priesthood that are not simply negative, concerned above all with excluding problematic personalities, but also positive, providing a balanced process of formation for suitable candidates, fostering holiness and the virtue of chastity. Saint Paul VI, in his encyclical *Sacerdotalis Caelibatus*, wrote that "the life of the celibate priest, which engages the whole man so totally and so sensitively, excludes those of insufficient physical, psychic and moral qualifications. Nor should anyone pretend that grace supplies for the defects of nature in such a man" (n. 64).

5. Strengthening and reviewing guidelines by Episcopal Conferences. In other words, reaffirming the need for bishops to be united in the application of parameters that serve as rules and not simply indications. Rules, not simply indications. No abuse should ever be covered up (as was often the case in the past) or not taken sufficiently seriously, since the covering up of abuses favors the spread of evil and adds a further level of scandal. Also and in particular, developing new and effective approaches for prevention in all institutions and in every sphere of ecclesial activity.

6. Accompaniment of those who have been abused. The evil that they have experienced leaves them with indelible wounds that also manifest themselves in resentment and a tendency to self-destruction. The Church thus has the duty to provide them with all the support they need, by availing herself of experts in this field. Listening, let me even put it this way: "wasting time" in listening. Listening heals the hurting person, and likewise heals us of our egoism, aloofness, and lack of concern, of the attitude shown by the priest and the Levite in the parable of the good Samaritan.

7. *The digital world.* The protection of minors must take into account the new forms of sexual abuse and abuse of all kinds that threaten minors in the settings in which they live and through the new devices that they use. Seminarians, priests, men and women religious, pastoral agents, indeed everyone, must be aware that the digital world and the use of its devices often has a deeper effect than we may think. Here there is a need to encourage countries and authorities to apply every measure needed to contain those websites that threaten human dignity, the dignity of women and particularly that of children. Brothers and Sisters: crime does not enjoy the right to freedom. There is an absolute need to combat these abominations with utter determination, to be vigilant and to make every effort to keep the development of young people from being troubled or disrupted by an uncontrolled access to pornography, which will leave deep scars on their minds and hearts. We must ensure that young men and women, particularly seminarians and clergy, are not enslaved to addictions based on the exploitation and criminal abuse of the innocent and their pictures, and contempt for the dignity of women and of the human person. Here mention should be made of the new norms *"on the most serious crimes"* approved by Pope Benedict XVI in 2010, which included as a new species of crime "the acquisition, possession or distribution by a cleric of pornographic images of minors…by whatever means or using whatever technology." The text speaks of minors "under the age of fourteen," but we now consider that this age limit should be raised in order to expand the protection of minors and to bring out the gravity of these deeds.

8. *Sexual tourism.* The conduct, the way of looking at others, the very heart of Jesus' disciples and servants must always acknowledge the image of God in each human creature, beginning with the most innocent. It is only by drawing from this radical respect for the dignity of others that we will be able to defend them from the pervasive power of violence, exploitation, abuse, and corruption, and serve them in a credible way in their integral human and spiritual growth, in the encounter with others and with God. Combatting sexual tourism demands that it be outlawed, but also that the victims of this criminal phenomenon be given support and helped to be

reinserted in society. The ecclesial communities are called to strengthen their pastoral care of persons exploited by sexual tourism. Among these, those who are most vulnerable and in need of particular help are certainly women, minors, and children; these last however need special forms of protection and attention. Government authorities should make this a priority and act with urgency to combat the trafficking and economic exploitation of children. To this end it is important to coordinate the efforts being made at every level of society and to cooperate closely with international organizations so as to achieve a juridical framework capable of protecting children from sexual exploitation in tourism and of ensuring the legal prosecution of offenders.[16]

Allow me now to offer a heartfelt word of thanks to all those priests and consecrated persons who serve the Lord faithfully and totally, and who feel themselves dishonored and discredited by the shameful conduct of some of their confreres. All of us—the Church, consecrated persons, the People of God, and even God himself—bear the effects of their infidelity. In the name of the whole Church, I thank the vast majority of priests who are not only faithful to their celibacy, but spend themselves in a ministry today made even more difficult by the scandals of few (but always too many) of their confreres. I also thank the faithful who are well aware of the goodness of their pastors and who continue to pray for them and to support them.

Finally, I would like to stress the important need to turn this evil into an opportunity for purification. Let us look to the example of Edith Stein—Saint Teresa Benedicta of the Cross—with the certainty that "in the darkest night, the greatest prophets and saints rise up. Still, the life-giving stream of the mystical life remains invisible. Surely, the decisive events of history of the world have been essentially influenced by souls about whom the history books remain silent. And those souls that we must thank for the decisive events in our personal lives is something that we will know

---

16   Cf. *Final Document of the VI World Congress on the Pastoral Care of Tourism*, 27 July 2004.

only on that day when all that which is hidden will be brought to light." The holy, faithful People of God, in its daily silence, in many forms and ways continues to demonstrate and attest with "stubborn" hope that the Lord never abandons but sustains the constant and, in so many cases, painful devotion of his children. The holy and patient, faithful People of God, borne up and enlivened by the Holy Spirit, is the best face of the prophetic Church, which puts her Lord at the center in daily giving of herself. It will be precisely this holy People of God to liberate us from the plague of clericalism, which is the fertile ground for all these disgraces.

The best results and the most effective resolution that we can offer to the victims, to the People of Holy Mother Church and to the entire world, are the commitment to personal and collective conversion, the humility of learning, listening, assisting, and protecting the most vulnerable.

I make a heartfelt appeal for an all-out battle against the abuse of minors both sexually and in other areas, on the part of all authorities and individuals, for we are dealing with abominable crimes that must be erased from the face of the earth: this is demanded by all the many victims hidden in families and in the various settings of our societies.

FINAL STATEMENT

FR. FEDERICO LOMBARDI, SJ, *President of the Joseph Ratzinger-Benedict XVI Foundation, Moderator of the Meeting*

We have heard the voices of the victims of the terrible crimes of sexual abuse against minors committed by members of the clergy. We sincerely ask them for forgiveness, as we do also of all our brothers and sisters, for what we did wrong and for what we failed to do.

We will return to our dioceses and communities in various parts of the world with a deeper understanding of this terrible scandal and the wounds it has caused on the victims and on the entire People of God. We recall what St. John Paul II said already in 2002, words that are still very current and express our commitment: "People need to know that there is no place in the priesthood and religious life for those who would harm the young." We want that absolutely all pastoral activities of the Catholic Church wherever they take place be completely safe for minors out of respect for their dignity and their human and spiritual growth.

Responsibility, accountability, transparency are the words that have resonated during these days in which we have prayed, reflected, and shared our experiences under the guidance of the Holy Father, Francis, and that we are committed to translating into concrete action. The collegial spirit and synodal journey of the ecclesial community will give us the support and encouragement needed to continue to overcome the tendency to hide things and to favor the institution over the persons it must serve. In this way, we can achieve spiritual and structural renewal necessary to root out from the Church every form of abuse, not only sexual, but also of power and conscience.

We are confident that from this Meeting concrete initiatives will soon follow. Among them:

- A new *motu proprio* from the pope "on the protection of minors and vulnerable persons," to strengthen prevention and the fight against abuse on the part of the Roman Curia and Vatican City State. This document will accompany a new law of Vatican City State and guidelines for the Vicariate of Vatican City on the same subject.

- The Congregation for the Doctrine of the Faith will publish a handbook that will help bishops around the world clearly understand their duties and tasks.

- In addition, in a spirit of communion with the universal Church, the pope has expressed the intention of creating *task forces* of competent persons to help episcopal conferences and dioceses that find it difficult to confront the problems and produce initiatives for the protection of minors.

- On Monday, 25 February, the Organizing Committee will meet with the heads of the Roman Curia who participated in this Meeting in order to ascertain the follow-up work now necessary regarding the proposals and the ideas decided upon during these days, as desired by the Holy Father.

These first steps are encouraging signs that will accompany us in our mission of preaching the Gospel and of serving all children throughout the world, in mutual solidarity with all people of goodwill who want to abolish every form of violence and abuse against minors.